ALSO BY JIM GRANT AND IRV RICHARDSON:

The Looping Handbook:
Teachers and Students Progressing Together
(with Bob Johnson)

Multiage Q&A:
101 Practical Answers to Your Most Pressing Questions
(with Bob Johnson)

Our Best Advice:
The Multiage Problem Solving Handbook
(with Bob Johnson)

BY JIM GRANT

A Common Sense Guide to Multiage Practices
(with Bob Johnson)

Developmental Education in an Era of High Standards
Every Parent's Owner's Manuals

(Three-, Four-, Five-, Six-, and Seven-Year-Old)
(with Margot Azen)

"I Hate School!" Some Common Sense Answers for Parents Who Wonder Why,
Including the Signs and Signals of the Overplaced Child

Retention and Its Prevention: Making Informed Decisions About Individual Children

VIDEOS BY JIM GRANT

Accommodating Developmentally Different Children in the Multiage Classroom

The Multiage Continuous Progress Classroom

Do You Know Where Your Child Is?
What Every Parent Should Know About School Success

Worth Repeating

To aid you, the child study team and parents, we have made many pages of this book reproducible.

Feel free to reproduce the Retention/Promotion Checklist, Checklist Summary Form, Individual Retention Plan, Individual Promotion Plan, and Appendices for educational purposes within your school.

(Not to be distributed for use between schools or throughout school districts.)

THE Retention/Promotion CHECKLIST

Jim Grant and

Irv Richardson

Crystal Springs
BOOKS

Crystal Springs Books
Peterborough, New Hampshire

© 1998 by Jim Grant and Irv Richardson

Printed in the United States of America

Published and distributed by:

Crystal Springs Books
Ten Sharon Road, Box 500
Peterborough, NH 03458-0500
1-800-321-0401

Publisher Cataloging-in-Publication Data

Grant, Jim 1942-
         The retention/promotion checklist / by Jim Grant and Irv Richardson.—1st.ed.
[128]p. : Ill.; cm.
Includes bibliography.
Summary: Provides educators with guidelines for making the decision to promote students
or keep them in the same grade for a second year. Includes instructions for the checklist,
information to help clarify the decision-making process and suggestions for ongoing student
support. The focus of the book is making retention and promotion decisions based on an
individual student's circumstances and needs.
ISBN 1-884548-20-2
1.Teaching. 2.Grade repetition. 3. Teacher-student relationships. I. Richardson, Irv, 1956- .
II. Title.
371.28—dc21 1998   CIP
LC Card Number: 98-71312

Senior Editor: Elizabeth Quinn
Editor: Aldene Fredenburg

Book and Cover Design: Susan Dunholter
Publishing Manager: Lorraine Walker
Type Compositor: Laura Courchene

Acknowledgments

The authors would like to thank the following individuals for
sharing their wisdom, expertise and guidance:

Ron Areglado, Anthony Coletta, Kelly Cunningham, Dick Dunning, Char Forsten,
Joe Hayes, Bob Johnson, Rob Lowe, Jeremy Lowery, Jim Uphoff, Lorraine Walker and
Jay LaRoche, who believed in the idea.

And special thanks to Elizabeth Quinn, without whom this book wouldn't be.
Thank you for the tenacity with which you approached this project. You challenged
us to clarify points which seemed fuzzy. You spent hours diligently editing and
rewriting to ensure everything was right. Your tireless devotion to a project which helps
teachers ensure that a child's school experience is the best it can be, is inspirational.

Dedication

To Susie, the first student I retained.
Susie is a success story; she is currently working as a registered nurse, is married
and has two children. She is living testimony that additional learning time works.
— Jim Grant

To Sabo and his mother Kathleen — who helped me to see that continuing a good
situation for another year can make a positive difference in a child's life.
— Irv Richardson

Contents

Introduction

The decision to promote or retain a child will affect him for the rest of his life. It's a decision with an intense short- and long-term impact on students and their families. It can create emotional devastation, or put a child on the path to success.

How can you be sure you are making the right decision for a student? How can you tell if an additional year in the same grade will hurt or help? How can you be sure that promoting this student will not mean continuing a cycle of failure?

Addressing these concerns is the focus of this book: How to make sensible, well-reasoned, and defensible retention and promotion decisions. Our goal is to help you reduce inappropriate retentions and promotions by judiciously selecting which students will benefit from an extra year and which will not.

This book isn't meant to provide a standardized format into which to fit each student; nor is it a diagnostic test to be scored, and the score used to make a retention or promotion decision. It is a common-sense approach to retention and promotion based on the authors' years of experience as teachers and principals.

We will introduce you to a variety of factors and circumstances and ask you to consider how they impact an individual student's performance. Each item on the checklist has been included as the result of consultation with principals, teachers, counselors, psychologists, and parents/guardians, and reflects their advice about what to consider when making critical retention/promotion decisions.

Each question is important; however, some may carry more weight than others. For example, chronological age at school entrance and developmental maturity often weigh heavily in the decision-making process, whereas the high transiency record of a military dependent may not.

Wrong Grade Placement and Retention

Grade-level retention is the most appropriate intervention for students whose problems in school stem from being in the wrong grade. These are students who are chronologically and/or developmentally at least a year behind their classmates in terms of their ability to meet the curriculum requirements for their current grade.

Even though grade-level retention is the best intervention for some students, until recently social promotion has been the standard practice. Grade-level retention was frowned upon for various reasons, from concern about the costs involved in providing an extra year of schooling for a student, to worry about the effect of grade-level retention on a student's self-esteem.

On the other hand, grade-level retention for students who are not developmentally immature, but instead are dealing with learning disabilities or other problems in their lives, can have a destructive effect. We hope this book will help you identify which students are developmentally too young for their grade, and which are facing other difficulties. Once you identify the problems facing your struggling students, you will be able to decide which interventions will help these students succeed.

Creating a Child Study Team

Retention and promotion decisions need to be made on an individual basis with input from a number of different sources. An excellent way to do this is to gather together a child study team of teachers, learning specialists, and parents/guardians, whose job it is to compile as much pertinent information as possible about each student and use the information to make a well thought-out decision.

We have made large portions of this book, including the checklist itself, reproducible to facilitate its use by a child study team. A copy of the checklist should be distributed to each member of the child study team. Each member of the child study team should familiarize himself with the questions on the checklist and answer the appropriate questions based on his relationship with the student.

When the child study team meets, one person is designated as the team leader and she is responsible for facilitating the discussion. Another individual is responsible for filling in answers from every team member on a single "master" checklist. This individual is also responsible for making sure that team members sign the checklist where appropriate.

If possible, parents/guardians should be present at all child study team meetings because the answers to some questions need to come from the parents/guardians. Please make it clear to them that the answers to these questions are confidential and are intended to help you make the best decision for their child. If the parents/guardians are uncomfortable answering some of the questions, omit them. Because the checklist is not meant to be scored, a few missing answers should not dramatically alter your decision.

Child study team members are encouraged to add their own questions they feel are important to the checklist. Examples of additional items might include number/age of siblings, sibling pressure, peer pressures, etc.

Once the checklist is completed, the child study team should discuss the answers, referring to relevant appendices, and use the information gathered to help make a decision to retain or promote the student. Once the decision has been made, the team should evaluate if the student needs the ongoing support of an Individual Retention Plan or Individual Promotion Plan. If this is the case, the team should work together to create a plan to ensure that the child receives the educational, psychological, medical, and social support he needs.

Goals of the Child Study Team

1. To involve the parent(s)/guardian(s) from the very beginning in all child study team meetings.

2. To determine whether or not the student should be retained or promoted by investigating all factors and circumstances that influence student performance and well being.

3. To discuss all alternatives to grade-level retention.

4. To recommend psychological or other testing when appropriate.

---

5. To provide and coordinate a wide range of support, including but not limited to, intervention programs, special services, as well as modifications and accommodations to the student's curriculum and instruction.

6. To create and implement an Individual Retention Plan or Individual Promotion Plan when necessary.

7. To assist the administration in making a grade-placement recommendation.

8. To provide professional support for each other.

9. To thoroughly document the retention/promotion process and procedure followed to arrive at a placement decision.

How To Use This Book

This book is designed as a work tool for teachers and administrators making retention/promotion decisions; as such, large portions of the book are reproducible.

The Retention/Promotion Checklist is made up of questions selected based on factors which educators and parents/guardians know make an impact on school success or failure. Some items are of a sensitive and personal nature and may cause parents/guardians to feel their privacy is being invaded. When this is the case, you should pass over these questions. School officials should work closely with parents/guardians to resolve any concerns that may arise. Remember, this is not a psychometric instrument, so leaving several items unanswered will not alter the decision-making process. The checklist is reproducible in its entirety.

The Checklist Summary and Recommendation pages are designed to help you quickly and easily summarize the reasons for your retention or promotion decision and the recommended course of action for the student. Once you have come to a decision to retain or promote a student, fill in the pros and cons of that decision on the summary sheet.

Parents/guardians are asked to sign the summary to show that they understand the team's recommendations and decision.

The Explanation of Checklist Responses will help you analyze and use the information you have gathered in the checklist. Each question's relevance to the retention/promotion decision is explained; the text also refers you to individual appendices in the back of the book which will either provide you with more specific information or ask you to answer questions that will provide further understanding of a student's difficulties.

The Appendices are designed to give you additional information to clarify your decision-making process. They are not intended to be used to identify or diagnose learning disabilities, behavior problems, mental or physical illness.

Although the answers to some questions in the appendices may indicate a potential problem, none of the appendices can replace the evaluation of a trained professional. When questions indicate, for example, that a student may have a learning problem, the appropriate response should be to refer the student for a complete evaluation.

Please keep in mind that none of the items in the appendices are absolutes. No single factor should be used to label a student or determine whether he is retained or promoted. The pages in the appendices are reproducible.

The Individual Retention Plan (IRP) and the **Individual Promotion Plan (IPP)** have been developed to help teachers, specialists, and parents/guardians come to a clear understanding of the goals, objectives and support services for an individual student. Teachers find these plans help them evaluate student progress and more clearly convey that progress to parents.

An IPP or IRP can also act as an early warning system of sorts because it includes follow-up deadlines for evaluating student progress. If this student is continuing to do poorly, the IPP or IRP can be adjusted or the retention/promotion decision can be reevaluated. These plans will help you establish goals for services, programs, accommodations and modifications, and create a review process to check the progress of each intervention.

Another important benefit of an IRP or IPP is that it gives parents/guardians a clear idea of what will be provided for their child, who is responsible for the intervention, and when they can expect to be updated on their child's progress. It is crucial that the document be shared with the parents/guardians, who must be involved in and support the school's decision, before the plan is implemented.

Samples of Completed Checklists and **Plans** have been included in this book to help guide your child study team. The students described in the samples have many of the problems and issues commonly associated with at-risk children. As you will see when you review the samples, retention/promotion decisions are not always clear-cut and require the cooperation of educators with different areas of expertise as well as parents.

Please note: *He* and *she* are used alternatively throughout this book with no distinctions. The gender identified in each response does not mean that a boy or girl is more likely to have this problem. The genders are used alternately to avoid the visually difficult he/she and his/her constructions.

The Retention/ Promotion Checklist

Some guidelines before you begin . . .

When using the checklist, make sure you record the name of the individual(s) who provided the answers.

A "yes" answer means this is true for this student.

A "no" answer means this is not characteristic of this student.

An "unsure" answer means you do not have enough information at this time to make a judgment.

N/A means it is not applicable to this student.

The Retention/Promotion Checklist

Student _____ Date of birth _____ Present grade placement _____

Name of person responsible for completing this checklist _____ Date _____

Child study team leader _____ Title _____

Parent(s)/Guardian(s) _____ Date _____

Directions: Where indicated, please list the name of the individual(s) who provided specific information. Please pass over any items that either you or the parents/guardians are uncomfortable answering.

1. What is your best estimate of this student's potential?

   ☐ High potential   ☐ Average potential

   ☐ Above-average potential   ☐ Below average potential

   ☐ Limited potential

2. Do you or the parents/guardians suspect that this student may be a "slower learner" (70–89 IQ range)?

   ☐ Yes   ☐ No   ☐ Unsure

3. Has this student's ability been evaluated with an individually administered IQ test?

   ☐ Yes   ☐ No

   If yes, what were the findings?_____

   _____

   _____

   _____

   _____

   Name(s) of the individual(s) who provided this information:

   _____ Date _____

   _____ Date _____

4. What is this student's basic academic skill level?

   ☐ Grade level   ☐ Below grade level   ☐ Unsure

   ☐ Well below grade level

   Please describe any areas of difficulty: _____

   _____

   _____

   _____

5. Does this student make a consistent effort to do his/her work?

   ☐ Always   ☐ Most of the time   ☐ Sometimes

   ☐ Seldom   ☐ Never

   Comments: _____

   _____

   _____

   _____

   _____

6. How would you describe this student's level of motivation?

   ☐ High motivation   ☐ Average motivation

   ☐ Low motivation

   Comments: _____

   _____

   _____

   _____

7a. Has this student been identified as learning disabled?

   ☐ Yes   ☐ No

   If yes, what is the nature of the disability?_____

   _____

   _____

7b. If the answer to question number 7a was "No," do you or the parents/guardians suspect that this student may have some type of unidentified learning problem?

☐ Yes   ☐ No   ☐ Unsure at this time

If yes or unsure at this time, please comment: _____

_____

_____

_____

_____

_____

Name(s) of the individual(s) who provided this information:

_____ Date _____

_____ Date _____

8. Do you or the parents/guardians have concerns about this student's ability to meet grade-level standards if the student is promoted to the next grade?

☐ Yes   ☐ No

If yes, please comment: _____

_____

_____

_____

_____

_____

Name(s) of the individual(s) who provided this information:

_____ Date _____

_____ Date _____

9. This student is a: ☐ Boy   ☐ Girl

10. Has this student ever skipped a grade?

☐ Yes   ☐ No

If yes, please indicate the grade level skipped. _____

11. Was this student an early school entrant (entered school underage)?

☐ Yes   ☐ No

12. What was this student's chronological age at the time of school entrance? _____ years _____ months

13a. Do you or the parents/guardians think this student's behavior is developmentally young for his/her chronological age in relation to same-age peers?

☐ Yes   ☐ No   ☐ Unsure at this time

If yes or unsure at this time, please comment: _____

_____

_____

_____

_____

_____

13b. Do you or the parents/guardians think this student's behavior is developmentally young for his/her present grade-level placement in relation to same-age peers?

☐ Yes   ☐ No   ☐ Unsure at this time

If yes or unsure at this time, please comment: _____

_____

_____

_____

_____

_____

Name(s) of the individual(s) who provided this information:

_____ Date _____

_____ Date _____

14. In your opinion, is this student assigned to the wrong grade?

☐ Yes   ☐ No   ☐ Unsure at this time

If yes or unsure at this time, please comment: _____

_____

_____

_____

_____

_____

15. Has this student ever had an extra year of learning time in any form?

☐ Yes   ☐ No

If yes, please indicate if this student:

☐ Stayed home an extra year

☐ Spent an extra year in a day care or preschool setting

☐ Took an extra year in a transition grade/program (i.e. pre-kindergarten, pre-first, pre-second, pre-third)

☐ Has already been retained in grade

☐ Remained an extra year in a multiage classroom

☐ Other (please specify) _____

Name(s) of the individual(s) who provided this information:

_____ Date _____

_____ Date _____

STOP - If this student has already had an additional year of learning time, retention is not an appropriate intervention. This child should be promoted and given support services; see questions 22-24 and refer to the Individual Promotion Plan (IPP).

16. Does this student exhibit signs and signals of school-related stress?

☐ Yes   ☐ No

If yes, check all stress signs and signals that apply:

At home – How often does this student:

	Often	Sometimes	Rarely	Never
A) Revert to bedwetting?	☐	☐	☐	☐
B) Not want to go to school?	☐	☐	☐	☐
C) Suffer from stomachaches or headaches, particularly in the morning before school?	☐	☐	☐	☐
D) Dislike school or complain that school is "dumb"?	☐	☐	☐	☐

If some of the areas checked were under "Often," please comment: _____

_____

_____

_____

_____

Name(s) of the individual(s) who provided information on Section A-D:

_____ Date _____

_____ Date _____

At school – How often does this student:

	Often	Sometimes	Rarely	Never
E) Want to play with younger children?	☐	☐	☐	☐
F) Miss school?	☐	☐	☐	☐
G) Complain about being bored with schoolwork, when in reality he/she cannot do the work?	☐	☐	☐	☐
H) Have difficulty paying attention or staying on task?	☐	☐	☐	☐
I) Have difficulty following the daily routine?	☐	☐	☐	☐
J) Seem unable to shift easily from one task to the next, one adult to the next, one situation to the next?	☐	☐	☐	☐

If some of the areas checked were under "Often," please comment: _____

_____

_____

_____

_____

_____

_____

_____

Name(s) of the individual(s) who provided information on Section E-J:

_____ Date _____

_____ Date _____

In General – How often does this student:

	Often	Sometimes	Rarely	Never
K) Become withdrawn?	☐	☐	☐	☐
L) Complain that he/she has no friends?	☐	☐	☐	☐
M) Cry easily and frequently?	☐	☐	☐	☐
N) Seem depressed?	☐	☐	☐	☐
O) Tire quickly?	☐	☐	☐	☐
P) Need constant reassurance and praise?	☐	☐	☐	☐
Q) Act harried/hurried?	☐	☐	☐	☐
R) Show signs of a nervous tic (i.e., frequent clearing of the throat, pulling out hair, twitching eye, nervous cough)?	☐	☐	☐	☐

If some of the areas checked were under "Often," please comment: _____

_____

_____

_____

_____

_____

_____

Name(s) of the individual(s) who provided information on Section K-R:

_____ Date _____

_____ Date _____

(Note: All children display some kind of stress at times. Severe stress is indicated when a child consistently displays several stress signs over an extended period of time.)

17a. What is this student's attendance record?

☐ Good attendance ☐ High absenteeism (15 or more days per year)

This student was absent ____ out of ____ school days.

17b. If this student has had high absenteeism, was it due to illness or disability?

☐ Yes ☐ No

If yes, please comment: _____

_____

_____

_____

_____

_____

_____

_____

18. Is this student's family highly transient (moved three or more times in five years)?

☐ Yes ☐ No

If yes, how often has the family moved since this student started school? _____

Student's History of School Difficulty

19. Has this student experienced serious difficulty in any of the following grades/programs? Please check all that apply. (N/A = Not applicable)

Day Care	☐ Yes	☐ No	☐ N/A
Preschool/Pre-K	☐ Yes	☐ No	☐ N/A
Head Start	☐ Yes	☐ No	☐ N/A
*Pre-kindergarten	☐ Yes	☐ No	☐ N/A
Kindergarten	☐ Yes	☐ No	☐ N/A
*Pre-first	☐ Yes	☐ No	☐ N/A
First Grade	☐ Yes	☐ No	☐ N/A
*Pre-second	☐ Yes	☐ No	☐ N/A
Second Grade	☐ Yes	☐ No	☐ N/A
*Pre-third	☐ Yes	☐ No	☐ N/A
Third Grade	☐ Yes	☐ No	☐ N/A
Fourth Grade	☐ Yes	☐ No	☐ N/A
Fifth Grade	☐ Yes	☐ No	☐ N/A
Sixth Grade	☐ Yes	☐ No	☐ N/A

* *Transition Grades/Programs*

Other _____

If yes to any of the above, please comment: _____

_____

_____

_____

_____

_____

_____

_____

Name(s) of the individual(s) who provided this information:

_____ Date _____

_____ Date _____

20. Does this student speak English as a second language or have limited English proficiency?

☐ Yes ☐ No

If yes, does or has this student received ESL/LEP support services?

☐ Yes ☐ No

29. Has this child ever been exposed to toxic substances such as lead, pesticides, inhalants, etc.?

☐ Yes   ☐ No

If yes, please comment: _____

_____

_____

_____

_____

Name(s) of the individual(s) who provided this information:
_____ Date _____

_____ Date _____

30. Do you or the parents/guardians suspect this student has:

Vision problems?   ☐ Yes   ☐ No   ☐ Unsure

Auditory problems?   ☐ Yes   ☐ No   ☐ Unsure

If yes or unsure, please comment: _____

_____

_____

_____

_____

_____

Name(s) of the individual(s) who provided this information:
_____ Date _____

_____ Date _____

31. Does this student have a serious physical disability?

☐ Yes   ☐ No

If yes, please comment: _____

_____

_____

_____

_____

_____

Name(s) of the individual(s) who provided this information:
_____ Date _____

_____ Date _____

32. Does this student's family live at or below the poverty level?

☐ Yes   ☐ No

If yes, please comment: _____

_____

_____

_____

_____

Name(s) of the individual(s) who provided this information:
_____ Date _____

_____ Date _____

33. Was this child's birth considered traumatic/difficult?

☐ Yes   ☐ No

If yes, please comment: _____

_____

_____

_____

Name(s) of the individual(s) who provided this information:
_____ Date _____

_____ Date _____

34. Was this child born with a low birthweight?

☐ Yes   ☐ No

If yes, please check:

☐ Low birthweight (5.5 lbs. or less)

☐ Very low birthweight (approximately 3.5 lbs. or less)

Comments: _____

_____

_____

_____

Name(s) of the individual(s) who provided this information:
_____ Date _____

_____ Date _____

35. Was this child born prematurely?

☐ Yes ☐ No

If yes, please check:

☐ Premature

☐ Extremely premature (approximately 25 weeks or less)

Comments: _____

_____

_____

_____

_____

_____

_____

Name(s) of the individual(s) who provided this information:

_____ Date _____

_____ Date _____

36. During the pregnancy, was the mother:
(check all that apply)

A. ☐ Abusing drugs/alcohol?

B. ☐ Smoking/exposed to secondhand smoke?

C. ☐ Malnourished?

D. ☐ Exposed to toxic substances (i.e., lead, pesticides, inhalants, etc.)?

E. ☐ Experiencing extreme stress (i.e., traumatized by divorce, abuse, poverty, etc.)?

F. ☐ Other (please specify): _____

Please comment on any factors or circumstances checked: _____

_____

_____

_____

_____

_____

_____

Name(s) of the individual(s) who provided this information:

_____ Date _____

_____ Date _____

37. Has this child ever suffered from malnutrition?

☐ Yes ☐ No

If yes, please comment: _____

_____

_____

_____

_____

_____

_____

_____

Name(s) of the individual(s) who provided this information:

_____ Date _____

_____ Date _____

38. Has this child had a traumatic experience such as:

Someone close to the child has died?

☐ Yes ☐ No

The child has witnessed or has been the victim of a violent act?

☐ Yes ☐ No

The child's family was or is in crisis?
(For example, going through a divorce)

☐ Yes ☐ No

Moving to a new home?

☐ Yes ☐ No

Someone close to the child was (or is) terminally ill or injured?

☐ Yes ☐ No

Other (please specify) _____

If yes to any of the above, please comment: _____

_____

_____

_____

_____

_____

_____

Name(s) of the individual(s) who provided this information:

_____ Date _____

_____ Date _____

39a. Do you or the parents/guardians suspect this child may be suffering from depression?

☐ Yes   ☐ No   ☐ Unsure at this time

If unsure at this time, please comment: _____

_____

_____

_____

39b. If the answer to question number 39a was "Yes," what signs of depression does this child display?

Often seems sad	☐ Yes	☐ No
Does not seem to have fun or enjoy school	☐ Yes	☐ No
Does not want to participate in activities	☐ Yes	☐ No
Prefers to be alone	☐ Yes	☐ No
Lacks enthusiasm	☐ Yes	☐ No

Please comment: _____

_____

_____

_____

_____

Name(s) of the individual(s) who provided this information:

_____ Date _____

_____ Date _____

40. Have you or the parents/guardians noticed this student displaying any signs of emotional problems such as:

Frequent, uncontrollable outbursts?   ☐ Yes ☐ No

Withdrawn, unable to relate to others?   ☐ Yes ☐ No

Frequent lying to parents/guardians?   ☐ Yes ☐ No

Other? _____

If yes, please comment: _____

_____

_____

_____

_____

Name(s) of the individual(s) who provided this information:

_____ Date _____

_____ Date _____

41. Do you or the parents/guardians think this student exhibits any serious behavior problems such as:

Frequent defiance of adults?	☐ Yes	☐ No
Aggressive/violent behavior towards others?	☐ Yes	☐ No
Frequent use of inappropriate language?	☐ Yes	☐ No

Other? (please specify) _____

If yes, please comment: _____

_____

_____

_____

_____

_____

Name(s) of the individual(s) who provided this information:

_____ Date _____

_____ Date _____

42. Do you or the parents/guardians feel this student exhibits signs of social problems such as:

Being unable to make or keep friends?	☐ Yes	☐ No
Does not get along with his/her peer group?	☐ Yes	☐ No
Has difficulty sharing/taking turns?	☐ Yes	☐ No
Tends to say or do inappropriate things?	☐ Yes	☐ No

If yes, please comment: _____

_____

_____

_____

_____

Name(s) of the individual(s) who provided this information:

_____ Date _____

_____ Date _____

43. What other issues should the child study team consider (siblings, is this a foster child, etc.)? _____

_____

_____

_____

_____

_____

End of Optional Health/Well-Being Questions

44. What is this student's attitude toward remaining at the same grade level an additional year?

Student supports staying at the same grade level for an additional year.

☐ Yes ☐ No ☐ Unsure at this time

Student is opposed to staying at the same grade level for an additional year.

☐ Yes ☐ No ☐ Unsure at this time

Comments: _____

_____

_____

_____

_____

_____

_____

45. What is this student's attitude toward being promoted to the next grade?

Student supports being promoted to the next grade.

☐ Yes ☐ No ☐ Unsure at this time

Student is opposed to being promoted to the next grade.

☐ Yes ☐ No ☐ Unsure at this time

Comments: _____

_____

_____

_____

_____

_____

_____

46. How do the parents/guardians feel about having their child remain at the same grade level for an additional year?

☐ They support their child remaining at the same grade level an additional year.

☐ They are unsure at this time about having their child remain at the same grade level an additional year.

☐ They are opposed to having their child remain at the same grade level an additional year.

Comments: _____

_____

_____

_____

_____

_____

_____

Name(s) of the individual(s) who provided this information:

_____ Date _____

_____ Date _____

47. How do the parents/guardians feel about their child being promoted?

☐ They support their child being promoted to the next grade.

☐ They are unsure at this time about having their child being promoted to the next grade.

☐ They are opposed to having their child promoted to the next grade.

Comments: _____

_____

_____

_____

_____

_____

_____

Name(s) of the individual(s) who provided this information:

_____ Date _____

_____ Date _____

48. The child study team members believe that this student should be:

☐ Promoted ☐ Retained ☐ Unsure at this time

Principal _____

☐ Promoted ☐ Retained ☐ Unsure at this time

Teacher _____

☐ Promoted ☐ Retained ☐ Unsure at this time

School counselor _____

☐ Promoted ☐ Retained ☐ Unsure at this time

School psychologist _____

☐ Promoted ☐ Retained ☐ Unsure at this time

Learning specialist _____

☐ Promoted ☐ Retained ☐ Unsure at this time

Child study team leader _____

☐ Promoted ☐ Retained ☐ Unsure at this time

Other _____

☐ Promoted ☐ Retained ☐ Unsure at this time

Other _____

☐ Promoted ☐ Retained ☐ Unsure at this time

Other _____

Comments: _____
_____
_____
_____

RECOMMENDATION

49. The child study team recommends that this student:

A. ☐ Be promoted to the next grade level and receive support services such as remediation, accelerated learning, summer school, etc.

B. ☐ Be promoted to the next grade level and stay with the same teacher in a looping configuration.

C. ☐ Be placed in a transition grade/program (i.e., pre-kindergarten, pre-first, pre-second, pre-third).

D. ☐ Remain another year at the same grade level with the same teacher.

E. ☐ Remain another year at the same grade level, but with a different teacher.

F. ☐ Remain another year at the same grade level, but in a different school setting. (This option may not be possible in some school systems.)

G. ☐ Remain an additional year in a multiage classroom.

H. ☐ Be placed back one grade level mid-year.

I. ☐ Other (please specify): _____

_____
_____

Comments: _____
_____
_____
_____
_____
_____
_____

50. The child study team is encouraged to create and implement either an Individual Retention Plan (IRP) or Individual Promotion Plan (IPP) for this student. This good faith plan is a non-binding, non-legal agreement created by the child study team focusing on identified goals to ensure school success for this student. This individual plan outlines a course of action that specifies what intervention programs, services and adaptations will be implemented, and who will take responsibility to see that they happen as well as when they will happen. **The child study team recommends an:**

☐ Individual Retention Plan ☐ Individual Promotion Plan ☐ IRP/IPP is not necessary at this time.

If a plan is to be created and implemented, who will be the child study team person responsible for managing the plan?

_____
Name   Title/Role

The child study team will meet again on _____ **to follow up on this student's progress.**

Retention / Promotion Checklist:
Summary & Recommendations

> The following summary is based on information and observations from the checklist, as documented by parents/guardians and school personnel.
>
> The school believes student placement decisions should be made on an informed, individual basis.
>
> Any decision will have pros and cons for the student. These factors are weighed out to make a placement recommendation that is in the best interest of the individual student. Along with the placement recommendation, an Individual Retention Plan (IRP) or an Individual Promotion Plan (IPP) is included where appropriate. The IRP or IPP is a plan of action for each student which includes program interventions and services, including instructional accommodations and curriculum modifications.

Student Name:_____ Date: _____ School Year: _____

Placement Recommendation: (see attached summary)

☐ **Retention**   **Individual Retention Plan**   Yes   No

☐ **Promotion**   **Individual Promotion Plan**   Yes   No

Next year's teacher: _____

_____

Summary prepared by: _____

_____

I/We accept/reject this recommendation:

_____
Signature of parent/guardian   Date

_____
Signature of parent/guardian   Date

Question No. 1 **What is the best estimate of this student's potential?**

Question No. 2 **Do you or the parents/guardians suspect that this student may be a "slower learner" (70–89 IQ)?**

Question No. 3 **Has this student's ability been evaluated with an individually administered IQ test?**

These questions help gauge whether the student is a slower learner. The needs of a slower learner are generally best met by promoting her to the next grade and keeping her with her agemates. Retaining a slower learner usually produces disappointing outcomes and may result in having an older, physically larger student in a classroom surrounded by younger, smaller, outperforming classmates.

In addition to promoting this student, the school should provide support services and make curriculum modifications and accommodations to her instruction as needed. These adaptations should allow the student to reach her potential without retention.

A slower learner who has missed a great deal of school because of illness or accident, adverse stress or trauma, or developmental or chronological immaturity is the exception. Under these circumstances, retention could provide a badly-needed additional year of growth which would maximize this student's achievement.

Please refer to:

Appendix A	Attributes of a Slower Learner
Appendix B	Factors Associated with Poverty
Appendix X	Auditing Your Retention/Promotion Policy: Practices 3, 4A, 4E, and 8

Question No. 4 **What is this student's basic academic skill level?**

This question helps identify children who are functioning academically below grade level. While such a student may be a candidate for retention, retaining a student having academic difficulties without identifying the cause of the difficulties puts him further at risk.

Many retentions are based solely on a student's inadequate academic performance. This practice is highly dangerous because these students are already at risk of failing school or dropping out. Reading one or more years below grade level in third grade, for example, is one of the major risk factors used to predict who will drop out of school.

If this student has not been diagnosed with a learning disability (and you do not suspect one is present) then the child study team needs to investigate the root cause of the student's academic deficiency. Some hard-working students of normal intelligence, taught by excellent teachers, may not become good readers until seven years old. The student may simply be a late learner, which means that some areas of the brain may have not developed enough to master the materials.

If the student is a late learner, then the next step is to provide him with appropriate experiences until he is ready to learn. Whether this means retaining or promoting him will depend on where his needs would be best met — in the same grade or the next.

If you retain the student, what will be different about his school experience during the second year? If the student is promoted, what can you do to support him so that he doesn't suffer increasing difficulties and fall further behind? For a student who is a late learner, some appropriate interventions might include:

- A different reading approach
- Instruction aimed at the student's learning style and reading style
- Direct phonics instruction
- Summer school
- Remedial reading
- One-on-one tutoring
- Placement in a multiage or looping classroom

Other reasons for a student's academic deficiency may be wrong grade placement, high absenteeism due to illness/accident, the presence of adverse stress/trauma, or developmental immaturity. When one of these issues is present, additional learning time in the same grade can be extremely beneficial to the student. If you choose to retain this student, you should also supply additional support services such as the ones outlined in Question 22.

 Please refer to:

Appendix X   Auditing Your Retention/Promotion Policy: Practices 4A and 5

Question No. 5   **Does this student make a consistent effort to do his/her work?**

Question No. 6   **How would you describe this student's level of motivation?**

If a student has low motivation, seldom or never makes an effort to do her work, lacks self-determination, or has a poor self-opinion, grade-level retention is not recommended. Retention is not an effective strategy to inspire an unmotivated student. Retaining a poorly motivated student may actually put her at additional risk.

A more appropriate course of action would be to promote the student and use interventions such as counseling services, an individual student contract, placement with a different teacher, or modifications and accommodations to her program and instruction.

Please refer to:

Appendix C   Indicators of Low Student Motivation
Appendix E   Signs and Signals of Depression
Appendix F   Signs and Signals of Poor Self-Concept
Appendix X   Auditing Your Retention/Promotion Policy: Practice 4L

Question No. 7a **Has this student been identified as learning disabled?**

Question No. 7b **If the answer to question 7a was "No," do you or the parents/guardians suspect that this student may have some type of unidentified learning problem?**

If the student has been identified as learning disabled and does not show signs of being developmentally young, then promotion with appropriate support and adaptations is recommended.

Some students who have been identified as learning disabled may also be developmentally immature. If this is the case, the child study team should provide the student with the necessary additional time to develop by recommending retention. This will enable the student to maximize his potential and help compensate for his learning difficulties. Retaining a student to correct a wrong grade placement will more closely align him with more appropriate curriculum and instruction.

Some children who are not considered learning disabled may be identified as "gray-area" students. Gray-area students often experience difficulty keeping up with schoolwork at their assigned grade level, and tend to be overwhelmed with their workload. It is appropriate to retain a gray-area student who is developmentally or chronologically young for her grade level placement. In this case, retention will provide a student with more appropriate age/grade expectations and demands. In addition to grade-level retention, the student will need math and reading support services. Every effort should be made to modify the student's program and make accommodations to her instruction.

If the student does not show signs of developmental, social, physical, or emotional immaturity, then retention will probably not be an appropriate intervention. The student should be promoted and receive support services, program modifications and instructional accommodations.

✔ Please refer to:

Appendix D	Spotting a Possible Learning Disability
Appendix G	Signs of Attention Deficit Disorder
Appendix H	Characteristics That May be Observed in Both the ADHD Child and the Crack-Exposed Child
Appendix K	Chronological Age Effect
Appendix X	Auditing Your Retention/Promotion Policy Practices 3, 4G, and 8

Question No. 8 **Do you or the parents/guardians have concerns about this student's ability to meet the school's grade-level standards if the student is promoted to the next grade?**

Promotion of a low-performing student has its place and is certainly appropriate under the right circumstances. A few examples of appropriate promotions include the following scenarios:

- Students who are already one year older than their classmates.
- Students who are slower learners (70–89 IQ).
- Students whose parents are adamantly opposed to retention or an extra year of time in any form.

If the child study team concludes that retention is not in the student's best interest, promotion to the next grade level is in order. The student's program and instruction will need to be modified and accommodated to assist him in meeting grade-level standards.

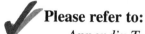 **Please refer to:**

Appendix T	Accommodation and Modification Ideas
Appendix X	Auditing Your Retention/Promotion Policy Practices 1, 4E, 9

Question No. 9   **Is this student a boy or girl?**

At school entrance, girls on average tend to be more developmentally mature than boys, sometimes by as much as six months. This means that a boy who just barely turned five on entering kindergarten could be not only substantially younger developmentally than a girl born on the same day, but much younger than girls who are both chronologically and developmentally older. Two children sitting next to each other in the same class could be 18 months apart developmentally, yet they are expected to perform and learn at the same rate. This may account for why boys are over-represented in the special education population, programs for the emotionally disturbed, grade-level retentions, remedial reading, remedial math, drop-out data, Title I services and the growing population of struggling learners.

Grade-level retention can be an excellent intervention to equalize education for developmentally immature students, particularly boys. If retained for appropriate reasons and at the appropriate time, boys can use this extra year to mature and grow. Please note that retention, especially for this reason, is far more effective with younger boys.

Although boys are more likely to show the effects of developmental immaturity upon school entrance, girls can also be developmentally and/or chronologically young, and can benefit from retention. Even though girls on average tend to be more developmentally mature upon school entrance, a developmental gap of a year or more can exist among girls in the same classroom.

Please refer to:

Appendix I	When Compared to Boys . . .
Appendix J	When Compared to Girls...
Appendix L	Ideal Minimum Chronological Age Range for Entering Each Grade/Program Level
Appendix X	Auditing Your Retention/Promotion Policy Practice 4H

Question No. 10   **Has this student ever skipped a grade?**

Question No. 11   **Was this student an early school entrant (entered school underage)?**

Question No. 12   **What was this student's chronological age at the time of school entrance?**

Some children are simply too young chronologically and are misaligned with their present grade level. Students who are underage for their grade placement because they skipped a grade or entered school early can generally be considered ideal candidates for retention if they are developmentally young. If a student is chronologically young for his present grade level because he was born during the last few months prior to the kindergarten entrance cut-off date, he can also be a good candidate for retention.

There are also other ways for a student to end up underage for his grade placement. A student born in the fall, who transfers from a school system with a December cut-off entrance date into a school system with a September cut-off date, could be considered underage for his grade. Some students are underage for their grade placement because their parents deliberately enrolled them in a private school with a late cut-off date and then transferred them into the public school system. This maneuver is sometimes used to bypass the local public school entrance policy.

✓ **Please refer to:**

    Appendix K   Chronological Age Effect

    Appendix L   Ideal Minimum Chronological Age Range for Entering Each Grade/Program Level

    Appendix M   Students Who Are Developmentally Too Young for Their Present Program or Grade Placement

    Appendix N   Signs and Signals of a Student Who is in the Wrong Grade

    Appendix X   Auditing Your Retention/Promotion Policy Practice 4M

Question No. 13a   **Do you or the parents/guardians think this student's behavior is developmentally young for his/her chronological age in relation to same-age peers?**

Question No. 13b   **Do you or the parents/guardians think this student's behavior is developmentally young for his/her present grade-level placement in relation to same-age peers?**

A student who is too young developmentally for either her chronological age or her grade level placement is a good candidate for retention. A "yes" answer to one of these questions could indicate that this student is a good candidate for spending two years in the same grade.

✓ **Please refer to:**

    Appendix K   Chronological Age Effect

    Appendix L   Ideal Minimum Chronological Age Range for Entering Each Grade/Program Level

Appendix M   Students Who Are Developmentally Too Young for Their Present
Program or Grade-Level Placement

Appendix O   Additional Signs and Signals of School-Related Student Stress

---

Question No. 14   **In your opinion, is this student assigned to the wrong grade?**

This is the single most important question on this checklist. An unequivocal "yes" answer would warrant, in most cases, having this student spend two years in the same grade, thus correcting her wrong grade placement.

It is common for underage students to feel isolated and complain of not having any friends in their grade. Often these students don't have the maturity necessary to experience success without undue school stress. Many bright underage students are able to do their schoolwork, but have difficulties in their social and emotional development. These developmentally young children may have problems in school that do not surface until years later.

Spending an extra year in the same grade can eliminate school stress associated with wrong grade placement and produce a much happier learner. If retention is warranted, the child study team should make sure this student receives additional support services if necessary. If, however, the parents/guardians of this student do not support an additional year in the same grade, you should not retain them. Some alternatives for this student include:

- Placement in a multiage classroom
- Tutoring
- Summer school
- After-school programs
- A "buddy system" or peer tutoring

These interventions will provide appropriate learning experiences and support for the student.

✓ **Please refer to:**

Appendix F   Signs and Signals of Poor Self-Concept

Appendix K   Chronological Age Effect

Appendix L   Ideal Minimum Chronological Age Range for Entering Each
Grade/Program Level

Appendix M   Students Who Are Developmentally Too Young for Their Present
Program or Grade Placement

Appendix N   Signs and Signals of a Student Who is in the Wrong Grade

Appendix O   Additional Signs and Signals of School-Related Student Stress

---

Question No. 15   **Has this student ever had an extra year of learning time in any form?**

If this student is already one year older than the classmates in his grade, then retention is inappropriate. Being retained in two grades increases the risk of a student dropping out. If you are considering an additional year of retention because this student is two years (or more)

developmentally behind his agemates, then you are dealing with more than a typical difference in development. Simply retaining the student for two years is not going to help him succeed. Instead, you should evaluate the child's needs and provide additional support services.

 Please refer to:

Appendix X   Auditing Your Retention/Promotion Policy Practices 9, 10A-E

Question No. 16   **Does this child exhibit signs and signals of school-related stress?**

The more signs and signals of stress a student exhibits, the more likely the student is either developmentally too young for his grade placement or has a potential learning problem. Serious concern is warranted if this student frequently displays multiple stress signs over an extended period of time. The student should be referred to a counselor to evaluate the causes of her stress.

 Please refer to:

For all of question 16:
> *Appendix O*   Additional Signs and Signals of School-Related Stress

For item 16H:
> *Appendix G*   Signs of Attention Deficit Disorder
> *Appendix H*   Characteristics That May Be Observed in Both the ADHD Child and the Crack-Exposed Child

For items 16E and L:
> *Appendix P*   Signs and Signals of Social Difficulty

For items 16E, K, L, M, N, P, Q, R:
> *Appendix Q*   Signs of Emotional Difficulty

For items 16K, L, M, N, O, P:
> *Appendix F*   Signs and Signals of Poor Self-Concept

For item 16N:
> *Appendix E*   Signs and Signals of Depression

Question No. 17a **What is this student's attendance record?**

Question No. 17b **If this student has had high absenteeism, was it due to illness or disability?**

Retaining a child solely because of high absenteeism is a dangerous practice. These students are already at risk to become school dropouts; retaining them may only increase the risk they will not finish school.

When faced with a chronically absent student (15 days or more a year) you need to first determine the cause. Is the student simply not showing up for school? If so, a more appropriate action would be to have the school truant officer, social worker or guidance counselor work with the parents/guardians to discover why the student stays away from school and to develop an attendance plan. If the parents/guardians are not willing to assist you, or if they contribute to the absenteeism, all the more reason to promote the student and provide support services. Retaining the student will not change her parents' attitudes, nor will it help the student. The result of retention will be an overage student, with a high rate of absenteeism, who is at risk for dropping out of school.

A student who has missed school due to a prolonged or repeated illness, or the result of an accident, is an exception to this practice. Such students are often good candidates for retention. The need to stay in the same grade another year because of a serious health problem is readily understood by the student and parents/guardians. An additional year of learning time under such circumstances will better help the student to achieve school success.

✓ Please refer to:

Appendix B   Factors Associated with Poverty

Appendix X   Auditing Your Retention/Promotion Policy Practices 4 I and 11H

Question No. 18   **Is this student's family highly transient (moved three times in five years)?**

The serious problem of transiency or "children in motion" cannot be solved by grade-level retention; it is not an appropriate solution for this problem. Transient students have special circumstances and are prone to drop out of school, tend to be poorly adjusted at school, have poor academic performance, and often require special education services. All of these problems require different interventions such as counseling, tutoring or remediation; grade retention was never intended to address any of them.

We recommend that highly transient students be promoted to the next grade level at the end of the school year and receive a full range of support services that match their unique learning problems.

An exception to this would be a student who is developmentally and/or chronologically young who moves frequently because a parent is in the military or has changed jobs. Such students are atypical and seldom experience the poverty and unstable family life often associated with transiency.

If the child study team believes this student's school difficulty is due to frequent moves as a result of job transfers or military postings, and is also chronologically and/or developmentally young, then an additional year in the same grade could be a beneficial way of putting this child at or near grade level.

✓ Please refer to:

Appendix B   Factors Associated with Poverty

Appendix X   Auditing Your Retention/Promotion Policy Practices 4J and 11E

Question No. 19 **Has this student experienced serious difficulty in any of the following grades/ programs?**

This is an important question because it helps reconstruct the student's school history. Past difficulties must be carefully evaluated for their causes and their effects on the student. If the student has a history of difficulty in past school or day care experiences, grade retention may be appropriate under the following circumstances and for the following reasons:

- The student's pattern of difficulty is the result of being developmentally or chronologically too young for his/her grade or program.
- The student is a late learner and needs additional time to learn required concepts.
- The student is physically underdeveloped and needs an additional year to grow and develop.

In each of the above cases, retention is the appropriate intervention to break the failure cycle.

If the student has had difficulty in earlier grades for reasons other than chronological or developmental immaturity, promotion to the next grade is appropriate. The child study team should develop an IPP for the student which includes recommendations for appropriate support services.

Question No. 20 **Does this student speak English as a second language or have limited English proficiency?**

Non-English speaking students often find themselves at a disadvantage in the classroom. Their lack of ability in English creates a serious barrier to instruction, and puts their education at great risk.

Many parents of ESL students request that their child take two years of learning time in the same grade to allow him to become more familiar with the English language. Another year in a strong ESL program could be beneficial to the student; however, it is important to realize that the problems confronting ESL students are due to communications difficulties, not because of wrong grade placement. If the student is not developmentally or chronologically young, a better solution than retention would be promotion in conjunction with strong ESL support which includes instruction in English.

Retention is recommended if the ESL student is also developmentally or chronologically young.

✔ **Please refer to:**

Appendix X   Auditing Your Retention/Promotion Policy Practices 4K and 11G

Question No. 21a Do you or the parents/guardians have reason to believe this student has a poor self-concept?

Question No. 21b If the answer is "yes" or "unsure at this time," do you or the parents/guardians believe this student's poor self-concept is directly related to the student's school difficulty?

If the child study team determines that this student has had a poor self-concept over a long period of time, retention will most likely have serious negative consequences. A better solution is to move the student up to the next grade level and provide counseling and other related services.

There are times when a student's poor self-concept is a direct result of the stress associated with wrong grade placement; if this is the case, retention may be an appropriate action. In these instances a student often regains her sense of self-worth very quickly when you remove the pressure of being in the wrong grade.

✓ Please refer to:
Appendix F   Signs and Signals of Poor Self-Concept

Question No. 22 Check all intervention programs and services that have been tried with this student to date.

In most cases, grade-level retention should be thought of as the intervention of last resort. It is important to try a wide range of interventions, programs, and services first. Be sure to accurately record the level of success achieved with each intervention program and strategy tried.

Before retaining a student, it is important to implement a variety of classroom adaptations and to provide additional support through school resources and programs.

Because the classroom teacher has the primary responsibility for a student's educational program, classroom adaptations should be made to ensure the student makes as much academic progress as possible. These classroom modifications can also provide optimal learning for the student.

When creating adaptations for the student, changes can be made in teaching strategies, what is required of the student and the conditions under which instruction takes place, including group size, time on task, time and duration of instruction, and lesson design.

Additional school programs such as Title I, peer tutoring, instructional aids, parent volunteers, etc., can add additional learning time and instruction for students who are struggling.

✓ Please refer to:
Appendix X   Auditing Your Retention/Promotion Policy, Practices 11C and F

Question No. 23 **What classroom accommodations and modifications have been made to date? Please comment on the results of these classroom adaptations.**

A student who experiences academic difficulty will need to have his program and instruction adapted to accommodate his learning style, developmental level, cognitive ability level and level of skills attainment. An Individual Retention Plan or Individual Promotion Plan should reflect past interventions and the results of these interventions.

✔ **Please refer to:**

Appendix T   Accommodation and Modification Ideas
Appendix U   Accommodation for Alcohol/Drug-Damaged Students
Appendix X   Auditing Your Retention/Promotion Policy, Practices 3, 11A, C, E, and F

Question No. 24 **Please list additional interventions, programs and services that will be provided for this student next year.**

Whether the student is retained or promoted, it is critical that additional support services be provided to help ensure the success of this intervention. Please note that many retained students not only need the extra time to grow and mature, but will also require additional academic support.

Some schools do not allow students to receive multiple services. Such artificial rules are wholly inappropriate, as many struggling students have learning problems that additional learning time alone can't solve. Retained students must be afforded whatever additional support is necessary to assure maximum success.

✔ **Please refer to:**

Appendix T   Accommodation and Modification Ideas
Appendix U   Accommodation for Alcohol/Drug-Damaged Students
Appendix X   Auditing Your Retention/Promotion Policy Practice 8

Question No. 25a **Is this student's physical development within the normal range for his/her age as determined by a physician?**

Question No. 25b **Do you or the parents/guardians think this student is physically average, small or large for his/her age?**

If this student is small for his age, it could be a physical sign of developmental immaturity. Other factors that hinder growth include lead poisoning, malnutrition, a serious medical problem, or family genetics. If there is concern about a child's small size, a pediatrician or other medical professional should be consulted to make a determination of the cause. Unusually slow physical growth may render a child incapable of succeeding in a particular grade unless he has more time to grow and develop.

If a student is physically small for his age it may make retaining the student easier. Physically small students seem to face fewer problems with retention because their smaller stature enables them to blend in better with their younger classmates. Because they are smaller, many times they are also expected to act younger.

Conversely, larger students are often expected to act older than their classmates even when they are chronologically younger. Retaining a student who is already larger than his peers and putting the student in a classroom of significantly smaller students will cause this student to stand out more than before. For these reasons, it is wise to be cautious when considering retention of a physically large student.

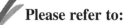 **Please refer to:**
    Appendix X   Auditing Your Retention/Promotion Policy, Practice 4D

Question No. 26 **Does this student have any serious medical problems?**

Question No. 27 **Has this student had any serious childhood illnesses?**

Question No. 28 **Has this student ever suffered a serious childhood accident?**

Some students not only have untreated medical problems, they lack access to medication and medical treatment. It is not uncommon for a serious or chronic illness to inhibit learning and development in a student. Chronic illnesses that restrict a student's interaction with peers — asthma for instance, precluding involvement in the physical rough-and-tumble of the playground — can also have a profound effect on the student.

A serious accident involving a long period of convalescence could also delay the student developmentally in all areas; it could also interrupt the child's normal physical pattern of growth.

In an article entitled "Factors That Influence Developmental Diversity," from the book *Every Child a Learner*, James K. Uphoff, Ed.D., stated,

> Any type of illness or problem which results in a passive child — in bed or just 'being very quiet' day after day — is more likely to result in a physically delayed development. Lack of body and muscle control can be a major problem for learners.

In some instances an allergic reaction to a food or other allergen can be mistaken for signs of hyperactivity. Having prior knowledge concerning a medical condition could prevent a needless referral for special education testing. The child study team should always explore health-related issues first when investigating why a student has school difficulties, and any medical problems should be addressed before considering retention.

In some cases, where illness has resulted in excessive absences, an additional year in the same grade can be an educational equalizer.

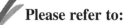 **Please refer to:**
    Appendix X   Auditing Your Retention/Promotion Policy Practice 4P

Question No. 29   **Has this child ever been exposed to toxic substances such as lead, pesticides, inhalants, etc.?**

Childhood exposure to harmful substances can cause severe problems such as birth defects, mental retardation, neurological disorders, brain damage, decreased growth, impaired hearing, and learning disabilities. Any one of these problems can lead to poor school performance. When combined with other factors, the risk of school difficulty multiplies for the student. A student with an extensive array of problems will require a corresponding number of interventions and support services which may or may not include retention.

Please refer to:

Appendix B   Factors Associated With Poverty
Appendix X   Auditing Your Retention/Promotion Policy Practice 4P

Question No. 30   **Do you or the parents/guardians suspect this student has vision or auditory problems?**

If the student has fallen behind in his schoolwork because of a previously undetected hearing or vision problem, then remedial support is recommended. Retention is not an appropriate intervention to address vision and/or hearing problems. Hearing problems in children can be a byproduct of repeated, untreated ear infections. The child may have difficulty hearing letter/sound relationships, and may in fact become a late reader. Parents/guardians who don't have medical insurance may suspect something is wrong, but do not have the money to pay for testing. If this is the case, your school may be able to direct them to the proper resource. (The Lions Club, for instance, runs a national program which provides prescription glasses for needy children.) Ideally, the student should be examined for hearing or vision problems and outfitted with glasses or a hearing aid if appropriate.

If you know a student has a vision or hearing problem, you will have to make accommodations for the child and plan your curriculum and instruction in a way that fully includes the student. Accommodations may include enlarged print, preferential seating or a classroom amplification system.

Question No. 31   **Does this student have a serious physical disability?**

A physical problem does not automatically warrant having a student spend an extra year in the same grade. However, under some circumstances students with a physical disability coupled with other factors and circumstances (such as a late birthday or developmental immaturity) may find that grade-level retention serves a useful purpose.

**Please refer to:**

Appendix X   Auditing Your Retention/Promotion Policy Practice 4P

Question No. 32   **Does this student's family live at or below the poverty level?**

Poverty can compromise a student's academic performance by depriving the student of experiences and opportunities to learn. It is recommended that you accelerate the learning of disadvantaged students with direct language instruction, after school tutoring and summer school to help make up for academic deficiencies.

Retention can be beneficial to a child living in poverty who is also chronologically or developmentally young by affording him a longer period of time to learn important concepts and skills. Students living in poverty can also benefit by being placed in a multiyear classroom, such as a looping or multiage continuous progress configuration.

Children from poor families can also benefit from smaller classes and all-day kindergarten programs. These children will require multiple programs and services over a long period of time.

Please refer to:

Appendix B   Factors Associated with Poverty

Question No. 33   **Was this child's birth considered traumatic/difficult?**

A traumatic birth may be one factor in a child becoming a "late bloomer" who may benefit greatly from additional time in a grade. According to Dr. James Uphoff, "A difficult birth can be an indicator of problems to come. When labor lasts a long time or is less than four hours, or when labor is unusually difficult, the child is more likely to experience problems. Long labor too often results in reduced oxygen and/or nourishment for the child just before birth. Some studies have found birth trauma to be associated with later emotional problems."

Question No. 34   **Was this child born with a low birthweight?**

A "yes" answer to this question may shed light on a possible reason for a student's difficulty in school. Low birthweight is associated with learning disabilities, a short attention span, health-related problems, developmental delays, overall low academic performance, grade-level retention, and school failure

For many children born with a low birthweight, additional learning time will prove very beneficial. Often additional interventions and services may be needed to address learning problems that time alone cannot fully meet.

Please refer to:

Appendix B   Factors Associated with Poverty
Appendix R   Babies Born with a Low Birthweight . . .

Question No. 35   **Was this child born prematurely?**

Premature babies have the same types of problems associated with low birthweight babies. Also, because of the nature of prematurity, most preemies are likely to be low birthweight babies. The lower the weight and the more premature babies are, the more likely they are to have learning problems. Gender is also a factor; at five years of age a boy who was born prematurely is more likely to have problems in school than a girl who was also born prematurely.

Prematurity can be a good reason to allow a student to stay in a grade an extra year. Other interventions and services may also be needed to address any learning problems the student may have.

✔ **Please refer to:**

Appendix B   Factors Associated With Poverty

Appendix R   Babies Born With a Low Birthweight

Appendix S   Advice on School Entrance Regarding Children Born Prematurely

Appendix X   Auditing Your Retention/Promotion Policy Practice 4P

Question No. 36   **During the pregnancy, was the mother abusing drugs/alcohol? Smoking/exposed to secondhand smoke? Malnourished? Exposed to toxic substances? Experiencing extreme stress?**

Prenatal exposure to a variety of influences can cause serious problems resulting in learning difficulties once a child enters school.

• Alcohol/drug abuse during pregnancy is associated with problems that can later affect a student's well-being, often throughout a lifetime. Serious problems directly related to alcohol abuse during pregnancy include mental retardation, limited or short attention span, speech and language deficiencies, prematurity, low birthweight, hyperactivity, learning disorders, stunted growth, and facial abnormalities.

• Cocaine and crack abuse are associated with prematurity, low birthweight, smaller head circumference, limited attention span, learning difficulties, behavior problems, and hyperactivity.

• Mothers who smoke during their pregnancy place their child at risk for low birthweight, asthma, physical growth retardation, hyperactivity, attention problems, slower cognitive development, and birth defects such as cleft lips and palates. Children who are exposed to secondhand smoke may miss one third more days of school, placing them at greater risk for school failure and dropping out of school. These children are also more susceptible to respiratory infections.

• Malnutrition during pregnancy can have an equally devastating effect on a child. As Dr. Ernest L Boyer reported in his groundbreaking book *Ready To Learn: A Mandate for the Nation*, "Fetal malnutrition affects up to 10% of the babies born in the United States. Damage to the fetus caused by poor nourishment between the twelfth and twenty-fourth weeks of gestation — a time most critical to brain growth — cannot be reversed."

• Prenatal exposure to toxic substances during pregnancy places both the mother and the unborn baby at serious health risk. Toxic substances can cause birth defects as well as learning disabilities in children.

• Extreme trauma and/or adverse stress can have a deleterious affect on both the mother and the unborn child. Examples include accidental injuries, exposure to measles, and infection with a communicable disease. Each of these examples can damage the unborn baby.

Please refer to:

Appendix B	Factors Associated With Poverty
Appendix G	Signs of Attention Deficit Disorder
Appendix H	Characteristics That May Be Observed in Both the ADHD Child and the Crack-Exposed Child
Appendix U	Accommodations for Alcohol/Drug Damaged Students
Appendix X	Auditing Your Retention/Promotion Policy Practice 4P

Question No. 37   **Has this child ever suffered from malnutrition?**

Children who are malnourished exhibit a variety of problems, all of which can negatively affect school performance. Signs to watch for include: an inability to concentrate, complaints of fatigue or lack of energy from the student, delayed physical growth, or symptoms of Attention Deficit Disorder.

Poor nutrition and deficiencies in a student's diet obviously cannot be addressed through retention. The school counselor and social worker should make every effort to address this serious health concern and continue to monitor and evaluate the student's progress. Many students may improve their academic performance once they are better nourished.

Please refer to:

Appendix G	Signs of Attention Deficit Disorder
Appendix X	Auditing Your Retention/Promotion Policy Practice 4P

Question No. 38   **Has this child had a traumatic experience?**

Students who have experienced a traumatic event in their lives or who are undergoing continual crisis in their home often become seriously depressed. They may need to be referred to a counselor, psychologist or social worker. You may need to make adaptations in the classroom that take into account their emotional overload.

Children exposed to violence are at great risk for profound emotional, physiological, cognitive and social problems. It is not uncommon for abused children to develop Post-Traumatic Stress Disorder (PTSD). The symptoms of PTSD include behavior problems, phobias, anxieties and depressive disorders.

Staying in the same grade with the same teacher for two years can be beneficial for an emotionally fragile student who has missed out on opportunities to learn because she was "shut down" emotionally. If you have the option available to you, it is recommended that traumatized students remain in a multiyear configuration such as a looping or a multiage continuous progress classroom.

Please refer to:

Appendix E   Signs and Signals of Depression

Question No. 39a   **Do you or the parents suspect this child may be suffering from depression?**

Question No. 39b   **If the answer is "yes," what signs of depression does the child display?**

Depression is becoming more common among elementary school children. Symptoms of depression may mask themselves as boredom or lack of motivation. Causes may include home or societal conditions, or a chemical imbalance within the child. A student who appears depressed should be referred to the family pediatrician or a psychologist for appropriate help.

If a student exhibits serious emotional problems, it can affect every aspect of his school life, including relationships with his classmates. The student should be given extra consideration in terms of being matched with an appropriate teacher, and may need counseling or special education assistance.

Please refer to:

Appendix E   Signs and Signals of Depression
Appendix F   Signs and Signals of Poor Self-Concept

Question No. 40   **Have you or the parents/guardians noticed this student displaying any signs of emotional problems?**

If this student has serious mental health problems, retention will undoubtedly add to her emotional difficulty. School officials are strongly urged not to use grade retention in this case. Retention is not a substitute for psychotherapeutic services.

More appropriate interventions for this student might include special education services or support services from the school guidance counselor, social worker or psychologist. If possible, assign the student to a teacher experienced in working with students with emotional problems. If a student's behavioral problems has created a rift between her and her classmates, moving the student to a new classroom with a new peer group will sometimes give a her a beneficial "fresh start."

If the school psychologist determines that the student's emotional upset seems to be school-related or school-induced (i.e. overwhelmed by too much academic pressure and stress), then retention may be a necessary move to extricate this student from an incorrect placement.

Please refer to:

Appendix P	Signs and Signals of Social Difficulty
Appendix Q	Signs of Emotional Difficulty
Appendix V	Traits of a Student with Behavior Problems
Appendix W	Traits of the Difficult Child
Appendix X	Auditing Your Retention/Promotion Policy Practices 4P and 8

Question No. 41 **Do you or the parents/guardians think this student exhibits any serious behavior problems?**

If this student has serious behavior problems, retention is not advised unless you believe school-induced stress is causing the problems. Retention is not a behavior modification program. Spending two years in a grade will most likely exacerbate the student's problems. More appropriate interventions may include:

- Special education services
- Support from the school guidance counselor/social worker
- Putting the student on a behavior contract with a teacher who demonstrates success working with students with behavior problems
- Moving the student to a new peer group

If the school psychologist determines that the behavior problems seem to be a recent issue with the student and feels the problems may be school-related or induced (i.e. overwhelmed by too much academic pressure with too many program demands) then retention in this case may be considered an appropriate intervention to reduce the stress underlying the problem.

Please refer to:

Appendix H	Characteristics That May Be Observed in Both the ADHD Child and the Crack-Exposed Child
Appendix N	Signs and Signals of Student Who is in the Wrong Grade
Appendix P	Signs and Signals of Social Difficulty
Appendix Q	Signs of Emotional Difficulty
Appendix V	Traits of a Student with Behavior Problems
Appendix W	Traits of the Difficult Child

Question No. 42 **Do you or the parents/guardians feel this student exhibits signs of social problems?**

Difficulty in getting along with one's classmates can be a sign of developmental immaturity. For example, developmentally young children may have trouble taking turns with other children, commonly get rejected by those children and may find school a very unpleasant experience. There's nothing more heartbreaking than children who are so out of sync with their schoolmates that they never get a birthday party invitation, are never invited to a friend's house, and are not included in play groups. If a student's social difficulty is clearly related to developmental youngness, retention in most cases can help put this student back on track socially.

If, on the other hand, the student's social difficulty is a reflection of his personality and temperament rather than developmental immaturity, retention will not help.

Please refer to:

Appendix P	Signs and Signals of Social Difficulty
Appendix Q	Signs of Emotional Difficulty
Appendix V	Traits of a Student with Behavior Problems
Appendix W	Traits of the Difficult Child

Question No. 43 **What other issues should the child study team consider? (siblings, is this a foster child, etc.)**

There are other factors which could impact the success of a retention or promotion decision. Members of the child study team are urged to share their concerns about these other factors. Some examples include:

• A second grade student with a younger sister in the first grade. Retaining the second grader will mean the siblings will be in the same grade. If there is sibling rivalry or competition between the two, every effort should be made to keep them with different teachers.

• Information on a student living in a foster home may be incomplete. This is something you will not be able to change. The child study team should be aware of this situation as they make a retention/promotion recommendation.

• If the school has a highly competitive academic environment, retaining this student could be harmful. The child study team is advised to look closely at the child's relationship with her peers.

Question No. 44 **What is this student's attitude toward remaining at the same grade level an additional year?**

Question No. 45 **What is this student's attitude toward being promoted to the next grade level?**

Retention is not an appropriate intervention for a student who is adamantly opposed to it. Forced retention will not produce the desired results; the student is likely to work against retention to prove it doesn't work. If the child study team recommends retention and the student strongly disagrees, the best solution is to promote the student and provide him with whatever support services he needs.

Many children have a surprising amount of insight into what is best for them, and actually support being retained, grateful for the opportunity to spend an extra year in the same grade.

If the student has been recommended for promotion and opposes moving to the next grade, this may be a sign that the child is feeling the stress of wrong grade placement. In this instance, the child study team should reassess the student's developmental readiness.

Keep in mind the student's age and maturity level; some children are obviously too young to judge their own best interests.

Question No. 46 **How do the parents/guardians feel about having their child remain at the same grade level for an additional year?**

Question No. 47 **How do the parents/guardians feel about their child being promoted?**

While a student's grade placement is the prerogative of the superintendent of schools, retention/promotion decisions must be mutually agreeable to both school officials and the parents/guardians. If the student's parents/guardians support a recommendation of retention, there is an excellent chance that additional time in the same grade will prove beneficial. However, if the parents/guardians are not solidly behind the recommendation, then retention is inappropriate, as it will not work without the necessary moral support. In this case, the student should be promoted.

In the same vein, if the child study team recommends promotion and the parents/guardians are opposed, this should raise a red flag. Parents/guardians who oppose promotion are probably in tune with their child's needs and difficulties in school, and generally would not support retention unless it was a necessity. Promoting a student against the wishes of her parents/guardians is problematic at best.

✓ **Please refer to:**
   Appendix X   Auditing Your Retention/Promotion Policy Practice l

Question No. 48 **The child study team members believe that this student should be . . .**

Question No. 49 **Recommendation: The child study team recommends that this student . . .**

Question No. 50 **The child study team is encouraged to create and implement either an IRP or IPP for this student.**

Making the correct retention or promotion decision is just the first step toward helping students; many students need additional assistance and support, whether they are retained or promoted. One very effective approach is creating and implementing an Individual Retention Plan (IRP) or Individual Promotion Plan (IPP) similar in nature to the plan used to help special-needs students. An IRP or IPP clearly outlines planned interventions, support services and programs. A blank IPP and IRP can be found beginning on page 73.

Appendices

These appendices are designed to give you additional information to clarify your decision-making process. They are not intended to be used to identify or diagnose learning disabilities, behavior problems, or mental or physical illness.

When an appendix indicates a student may have a learning problem, for example, the student should be immediately referred for evaluation. Although the answers to some appendices may indicate a potential problem, none of the appendices can replace the evaluation of a trained professional.

Please keep in mind that none of the items in the appendices are absolutes. No single factor should be used to label a child or determine whether he is retained or promoted.

CONFIDENTIAL

THE
Retention/
Promotion
CHECKLIST

Attributes of a Slower Learner *

Please check all attributes that apply to: _____ Date: _____
Student's name

Caution: Do not use this information to identify, diagnose or label any student a slow learner. This information is for discussion purposes only. The determination of a child's index of intelligence should only be assessed by trained personnel.

How often have you observed this student exhibiting the following behaviors:	Often	Sometimes	Rarely	Never
Frequently cannot recall detail(s) from memory				
Questions/comments reveal a lack of comprehension of new concepts				
Has difficulty following directions				
Becomes easily frustrated and upset when he/she doing his/her homework				
Takes an inordinate amount of time to complete his/her work				
Becomes confused when there are changes in routines or plans				
Becomes easily distracted when attempting school work				
Has difficulty focusing on a specific task				
Has difficulty sustaining attention to verbal explanations				
Complains about too much schoolwork				
Complains about not having enough time to do his/her school work				
Becomes easily confused about the rules to games				
Tends to be a spectator rather than a participant in activities				
Follows the lead of others; has difficulty remembering classroom routines				

Note: None of these attributes of a slower learner are absolutes; many students may display a few attributes of a slower learner at times. Serious concern may be warranted when a student exhibits multiple attributes of a slower learner. If the "often" column is checked repeatedly, the child study team should create and implement an Individual Retention Plan or Individual Promotion Plan (depending on its placement decision) to assure support for this student.

Certain attributes of a slower learner may also be indicative of other problems or conditions such as Attention Deficit Disorder, depression, school-related stress, learning disabilities, or developmental immaturity. If you believe this student is a slower learner, referral for a comprehensive evaluation should be requested immediately to determine the nature of this child's problem or condition.

Name(s) of the individual(s) who provided this information:

_____Title/Position _____Date_____

_____Title/Position _____Date_____

(*70–89 IQ)

Appendix B

For use with questions 1, 2, 3, 17a, 17b, 18, 29, 32, 34, 35, 36, 37

Factors Associated with Poverty

Children living at or below the poverty threshold:

- Experience a higher family stress level

- May lack health care

- Often experience unhealthy living conditions

- Often live in unsafe neighborhoods

- Are exposed to pollution more often

- Tend to have poor nutrition

- May have a lower IQ (extreme deprivation)

- Often have few available resources for learning (i.e., books, recordings, games, computer, etc.)

- Are four times more likely to be abused or neglected

- Often have inadequate clothing

- Are more likely to be exposed to secondhand smoke

- Are more likely to be exposed to an alcohol/drug environment

- Are more likely to be placed in a poor quality day care situation

- Are twice as likely to drop out of school

- Have a higher rate of juvenile delinquency

- Are five to seven times more likely to become pregnant as a teenager

- Are more likely to have excessive absences

- Have a higher incidence of giving birth to a low birthweight and/or premature baby

- Are more likely to have a family who is highly transient

Note: Poverty is one of the top five conditions limiting student accomplishments.

For use with questions 5, 6

Indicators of Low Student Motivation

Please check all indicators that apply to: _____ Date _____

Student's name

Caution: This information is strictly for discussion purposes.

How often have you observed this student exhibiting the following indicators of low motivation?	Often	Sometimes	Rarely	Never
Procrastinates				
Refuses to respond when urged to complete work				
Expresses he/she has lost confidence in his/her ability to succeed; sees no point in trying				
Expresses feelings of inadequacy (i.e. "I'm stupid," "I'm a SPED," etc.)				
Seems disinterested in most academics				
Seems apathetic about schoolwork in general				
Demonstrates little desire to work hard				
Displays a "can't do" attitude				
Spectates rather than participates in school activities				

Note: At times many students display some indicators of low motivation. Serious concern may be warranted if a student exhibits multiple indicators over an extended period of time. If the "often" column is checked repeatedly, then every effort should be made to reach and inspire this student. It would be helpful to brainstorm with fellow educators to develop ideas to help this student. Indicators of low motivation associated with the consequences of wrong grade placement may also be indicative of other problems such as learning disabilities, lower than average ability, depression, social difficulties, emotional difficulties, and behavior problems. None of the indicators of low student motivation are absolutes.

Name(s) of the individual(s) who provided this information:

_____Title/Position _____Date_____

_____Title/Position _____Date_____

© 1998 Crystal Springs Books • 1-800-321-0401

For use with questions 7a, 7b

Spotting a Possible Learning Disability

Please check all traits that apply to: _____ Date _____

Student's name

Caution: Do not use this information to identify, diagnose or label any student as learning disabled. The use of this information is for discussion purposes only. A diagnosis of learning disabilities should only be made by a psychologist in conjunction with a pediatrician or family doctor.

How often have you observed this student exhibiting the following traits:	Often	Sometimes	Rarely	Never
Has difficulty recalling acquired knowledge				
Requires a number of repetitions of taught materials (rate of acquisition and knowledge retention are lower than those of age-appropriate peers)				
Depends on others to organize work for him/her				
Seems unable to discriminate between important facts and details or unimportant facts				
Seems unable to remain attentive and focused on classroom learning				
Experiences difficulty with language expression				
Experiences difficulty with receptive language				
Motivation for school work is low				
Struggles with social interaction				
Experiences difficulty applying information in new contexts				
Requires work load and time allowances to be adapted to specific need				
Exhibits poor social judgement				
Is easily confused by changes in schedule				
Is easily confused by verbal innuendo; misreads body language				

Note: Many students exhibit some of these traits at various times. Serious concern may be warranted when a student consistently displays many of these traits over a long period of time. If the "often" column is checked repeatedly, then referral for a comprehensive evaluation by a child psychologist should be requested to determine if this child has learning disabilities.

Certain signs of learning disabilities may be indicative of other problems or conditions such as Attention Deficit Disorder, depression, lower than average ability, behavior problems and school-related stress. None of these learning disability traits are absolutes.

Adapted from the work of Gretchen Goodman with permission. This chart was taken from the book *Our Best Advice: The Multiage Problem Solving Handbook,* by Jim Grant, Bob Johnson, and Irv Richardson.

Name(s) of the individual(s) who provided this information:

_____Title/Position _____Date_____

_____Title/Position _____Date_____

For use with questions 5, 6, 16N, 38, 39a, 39b

Signs and Signals of Depression

Please check all signs and signals that apply to: _____ Date _____
Student's name

Caution: Do not use this information to identify, diagnose or label any student as being depressed. This information is for discussion purposes only. Diagnosis and subsequent treatment for depression should only be provided by a medical doctor.

How often have you observed this student exhibiting the following signs or signals:	Often	Sometimes	Rarely	Never
Expresses a dislike for school				
Cries easily or frequently				
Has a pervasive mood of sadness				
Tends to be a loner with few friends				
Tends to be non-participatory in school activities				
Seems disengaged, unattached				
Seems not to care about his/her personal hygiene				
Tells you he/she has trouble sleeping				
Appears irritable, angry, or sullen				
Lacks enthusiasm about things in general				
Makes negative statements about the future				
Has excessive absenteeism				
Complains about being tired in spite of adequate sleep				

In extreme cases of depression, a child may exhibit self-destructive behaviors such as:

Bulimia/Anorexia	☐ Yes	☐ No	Talking about suicide	☐ Yes	☐ No
Pulling out hair	☐ Yes	☐ No	Alcohol/drug abuse	☐ Yes	☐ No
Digging/scratching/cutting of skin	☐ Yes	☐ No	Other	_____

A yes to any of the above areas indicates a top priority referral for this student.

Note: Many students display a few signs and signals of depression at times. Serious concern is warranted when a student displays multiple signs of depression over an extended period of time. If the "often" column is checked repeatedly, then this student should be referred to the school guidance counselor for services.

Certain signs and signals of depression may also be indicative of other problems or conditions such as social difficulty, poor self-concept, lower than average ability, school-related stress, emotional difficulty, behavior problems, Attention Deficit Disorder, and learning disabilities. None of these signs and signals of depression are absolutes.

Name(s) of the individual(s) who provided this information:

_____Title/Position _____Date_____

_____Title/Position _____Date_____

For use with questions 5, 6, 14, 16K-P, 21a, 21b, 39a, 39b

Signs and Signals of Poor Self-Concept

Please check all signs and signals that apply to: _____ Date _____

Student's name

How often have you observed this student exhibiting the following signs or signals of having a poor self-concept:	Often	Sometimes	Rarely	Never
Disengages from social interaction				
Expresses negative self-talk ("I can't do that as well as the other kids")				
Expresses feelings of not belonging				
Lacks self-confidence				
Avoids participating in group activities				
Expresses concern about being inferior to the other students				
Prefers individual sports to team sports				
Seems fearful and insecure				
Exhibits poor personal hygiene				
Gives up easily				
Seems intolerant of others				
Tends to be an unmotivated learner				
Resists trying new things				
Makes little sustained eye contact				
Tends to be a spectator rather than a participant				
Avoids responsibility for behavior				
Can be disrespectful to others				
Becomes verbally/physically abusive to others				
Resists authority				
Becomes angry with little provocation				

Note: Almost all students display some signs and signals of poor self-concept at times. Serious concern may be warranted when a student exhibits multiple signs and signals of poor self-concept over an extended period of time. Certain signs and signals of poor self-concept may also be indicative of other problems or conditions, such as depression, emotional difficulties, or social difficulties. If the "often" column is checked repeatedly, then the student should be referred to the school guidance counselor for services.

Name(s) of the individual(s) who provided this information:

_____Title/Position _____Date_____

_____Title/Position _____Date_____

Appendix G

CONFIDENTIAL

THE
**Retention/
Promotion**
CHECKLIST

For use with questions 7a, 7b, 16H, 36, 37

Signs of Attention Deficit Disorder

Please check all signs that apply to: _____ Date _____
Student's name

Caution: Do not use this information to identify, diagnose or label any student as having ADD. This information is for discussion purposes only. A diagnosis of ADD/ADHD should only be made by a medical doctor.

How often have you observed this student exhibiting the following behaviors:	Often	Sometimes	Rarely	Never
Calls out in class when asked not to				
Forgets items				
Daydreams or "spaces out"				
Has difficulty focusing on a single task				
Becomes impatient				
Has difficulty delaying gratification				
School work is done with little care				
Exhibits poor fine motor control in handwriting				
Loses things (toys, clothes, books, etc.)				
Tends to be in constant motion				
Is easily discouraged				
Lacks self-control				
Appears disorganized				
Exhibits inattentiveness				
Has difficulty completing all aspects of a task				
Easily distracted by external stimuli				

Note: Many students may display some of these signs at times. Serious concern is warranted when a student exhibits multiple signs of ADD over an extended period of time. Some of these signs of ADD may also be indicative of other problems or conditions such as depression, emotional difficulty, developmental immaturity, or lower than average ability. If the "often" column has been checked repeatedly, then the student should be referred for a comprehensive evaluation.

Name(s) of the individual(s) who provided this information:

_____Title/Position _____Date_____

_____Title/Position _____Date_____

Appendix H

For use with questions 7a, 7b, 16H, 36, 41

Characteristics That May be Observed in Both the ADHD Child and the Crack-Exposed Child

The child:

- Often fidgets or squirms in his/her seat

- Has difficulty remaining seated when asked to do so

- Is easily distracted by extraneous stimuli

- Has difficulty awaiting turns in games or in group settings

- Often blurts out answers before a question is complete

- Has difficulty following instructions

- Often shifts from one incomplete activity to another

- Has difficulty playing quietly

- May talk excessively

- Often interrupts or intrudes on others

- Often does not seem to listen when spoken to

- Often loses things needed for assignments

- Often engages in physically dangerous activities

- May become too focused on one task to the exclusion of all other stimuli

Other characteristics that may also be quite common to both groups of children include: visual and auditory perception disabilities, integration and memory disabilities, expressive language disabilities, and problems with gross motor control and coordination. Teachers may also observe distractibility, hyperactivity, and impulsivity, as well as immaturity, social disabilities, and performance inconsistency.

Source: Adapted with permission from *Kids, Crack and the Community: Reclaiming Drug Exposed Infants and Children*, by Barbara Barrett Hicks, Copyright 1993 by the National Education Service, 1252 Loesch Road, PO Box 8, Bloomington, Indiana 47402, 1-800-733-6786.

Appendix I

For use with question 9

When Compared to Boys . . .

Girls entering kindergarten are more likely to:

- Hold a pencil correctly

- Button their clothes

- Write or draw rather than scribble

- Be able to identify more colors

- Count to 20 or beyond

- Write their own names

- Recognize more letters of the alphabet

- Have a longer attention span

- Fidget less than boys

- Show an interest in reading

- Have speech understandable to a stranger

- Not stutter or stammer

Appendix J

For use with question 9

When Compared to Girls . . .

Substantially more boys than girls are:

- "Late bloomers"

- Identified as learning disabled

- Identified as Attention Deficit Hyperactivity Disorder (ADHD)

- Language-delayed

- Identified as Attention Deficit Disorder (ADD)

- Enrolled in support services (i.e., Title I, Remedial Math/Reading)

- Late readers

- School drop-outs

- Retained in grade

- Failed in school

- Referred for discipline problems

- Struggling learners

- Placed in programs for the emotionally disturbed

Note: Many experts believe these gender discrepancies are due to the maturational growth differences between the genders. Please keep in mind that these statements are not absolutes.

For use with questions 7a, 7b, 10, 11, 12, 13a, 13b, 14

Chronological Age Effect

The chronologically younger children in any grade are far more likely than the older children in that grade to:

- Fail a grade

- Drop out of school

- Be referred for special services and special education

- Be diagnosed as learning disabled

- Be sent to the principal's office for discipline problems (even when in high school)

- Receive various types of counseling services

- Receive lower grades than their ability scores would indicate as reasonable

- Be behind their grade peers in athletic skill level

- Be chosen less frequently for leadership roles by peers or adults

- Participate in special service programs such as Title I

- Be in speech therapy programs

- Be slower in social development

- Rank lower in their graduating class

- Commit suicide

- Be more of a follower than a leader

- Be less attentive in class

- Earn lower grades

- Score lower on achievement tests

Note: None of these consequences associated with a late birth date are absolutes. There are always exceptions.

From: *Real Facts from Real Schools: School Readiness and Transition Programs* by James K. Uphoff, Ed.D. © 1995 by Modern Learning Press, Rosemont, New Jersey.

Appendix L

For use with questions 9, 10, 11, 12, 13a, 13b, 14

Ideal Minimum Chronological Age Range for Entering Each Grade/Program Level

Note: The ages suggested below represent an ideal chronological age range for entrance into each grade/program level. Please keep in mind that these age ranges are recommendations and are not to be interpreted as absolutes.

Grade/Program	Boy	Girl
Kindergarten	5½ - 6	5 - 5½
Grade 1	6½ - 7	6 - 6½
Grade 2	7½ - 8	7 - 7½
Grade 3	8½ - 9	8 - 8½
Grade 4	9½ - 10	9 - 9½
Grade 5	10½ - 11	10 - 10½
Grade 6	11½ - 12	11 - 11½
Grade 7	12½ - 13	12 - 12½
Grade 8	13½ - 14	13 - 13½

Appendix M

For use with questions 10, 11, 12, 13a, 13b, 14

Students Who are Developmentally Too Young for Their Present Program or Grade Level Placement:

- Are often chronologically young

- Are often male

- Tend to be socially inept

- Tend to be emotionally immature

- May be physically less developed for his/her chronological age

- May be cognitively unaware

These factors can greatly influence a student's chance to reach full potential and long-term school success.

For use with question 10, 11, 12, 14, 41

Signs and Signals of a Student Who is in the Wrong Grade

Please check all indicators of wrong
grade placement that apply to: _____   _____
Student's name   Date

How often have you observed this student exhibiting the following signs of wrong grade placement:	Often	Sometimes	Rarely	Never
Behavior problems				
Has difficulty paying attention				
Demonstrates difficulty learning routine tasks				
Has high absenteeism				
Exhibits characteristics of a learning-disabled student				
Exhibits persistent low academic performance				
Behaves impulsively				
Has low self-confidence				
Seems depressed				
Possesses a poor self-concept				
Is easily discouraged				
Is below reasonable grade-level expectations				
Has low physical and emotional stamina				
Displays poor decision-making skills				
Has difficulty socially				
And, in extreme cases, exhibits self-destructive behaviors				

Note: Many of these children require remedial and counseling services as a direct result of being
in the wrong grade. None of the signs and signals of wrong grade placement are absolutes.

Name(s) of the individual(s) who provided this information:

_____Title/Position _____Date_____

_____Title/Position _____Date_____

For use with questions 13a, 13b, 14, 16

Additional Signs and Signals of School-Related Student Stress

Please check all signs and signals that apply to:_____ Date_____
Student's name

How often have you observed this student exhibiting the following signs of school stress:	Often	Sometimes	Rarely	Never
Behavior problems				
Aggressive behavior				
Engages in negative self-talk				
Shows little interest in academics				
Has trouble finishing his/her work				
Exhibits persistently low academic performance				
Behaves impulsively				
Seems unmotivated				
Exhibits a poor self-concept				
Is easily discouraged				
Exhibits low physical and emotional stamina				
Displays poor decision-making skills				
Exhibits difficulty in social situations				
Is off-task				
Exhibits self-destructive behaviors				
Complains about too much school work				
Seems to not take his/her school work seriously				

Note: All students display some signs and signals of school-related stress at times. Serious concern may be warranted if a student exhibits multiple stress signs over an extended period of time. Many of these stress signs and signals may also be indicative of other problems such as: learning disabilities, depression, social difficulties, emotional difficulties, and a slow learner or student with behavior problems. If the "often" column is checked repeatedly, then this student should be referred to the school counselor for services.

Name(s) of the individual(s) who provided this information:

_____Title/Position _____Date_____

_____Title/Position _____Date_____

For use with questions 16E, 16L, 40, 41, 42

Signs and Signals of Social Difficulty

Please check all signs and signals that apply to: _____ Date _____
                                                          Student's name

How often have you observed this student exhibiting the following signs or signals of social difficulty:	Often	Sometimes	Rarely	Never
Has problems making friends				
Has difficulty sustaining a friendship over time				
Is excluded from activities by other children				
Lacks a sense of propriety				
Does or says the wrong thing for the situation				
Is not invited to play with other children				
Is not invited to birthday parties or sleepovers				
Violates the personal space of other children				
Has problems sharing, taking turns, or trading off				
Has difficulty working cooperatively with other children				
Prefers playing with younger children				
Prefers adult company				
Experiences difficulty sharing a conversation with peers				
Steals from other children				

Note: Many students display some signs and signals of social difficulty at times. Serious concern is warranted when a student displays multiple signs over an extended period of time. If the "often" column is checked repeatedly, then this student should be referred to the school guidance counselor for services. Certain signs and signals of social difficulty may also be indicative of other problems or conditions such as depression, low self-concept, school-related stress, emotional difficulty, behavior problems, and developmental immaturity. None of these signs and signals of social difficulty are absolutes.

Name(s) of the individual(s) who provided this information:

_____Title/Position _____Date_____

_____Title/Position _____Date_____

For use with questions 16E, K, L, M, N, P, Q, R, 40, 41, 42

Signs of Emotional Difficulty

Please check all signs that apply to: ⎯⎯⎯⎯⎯⎯⎯⎯⎯⎯⎯⎯⎯⎯ Date⎯⎯⎯⎯⎯⎯
Student's name

Caution: Do not use this information to identify, diagnose or label any student as emotionally disturbed. This information is for discussion purposes only. A diagnosis of emotional disturbance should only be made by a psychologist or psychiatrist in conjunction with a pediatrician or family doctor.

How often have you observed this student exhibiting the following signs of emotional difficulty:	Often	Sometimes	Rarely	Never
Irrational outbursts of anger and rage				
Has difficulty handling transitions (change of plans, substitute teacher, schedule change, etc.)				
Exhibits hostile behavior toward other students (kicking, biting, hitting, hair pulling, etc.)				
Speaks abusively to fellow students and/or adults				
Tells lies or makes up tall stories				
Says he/she is victimized or singled out for discipline				
Creates an incident to be the center of attention				
Is avoided by other children				
Exhibits inappropriate behavior for the situation				
Tends to be withdrawn				
Demonstrates difficulty relating to other students				
Tends to become emotionally fragile under normal school circumstances				
Takes things that don't belong to him/her				

Note: Many students display some signs of emotional difficulty at times. Serious concern may be warranted when a student exhibits multiple signs of emotional difficulty over an extended period of time. If the "often" column is checked repeatedly, then this student should be referred to the school counselor for services. It is also recommended that this student be placed with a teacher who is patient, tolerant, predictable, kind/understanding, a firm disciplinarian, and has been trained to work with special-needs students.

   Certain characteristics or signs may also be indicative of other problems or conditions such as depression, Attention Deficit Disorder, low self-concept, school-related stress, social difficulties, behavior problems, and developmental immaturity. None of these signs of emotional difficulty are absolutes.

Name(s) of the individual(s) who provided this information:

⎯⎯⎯⎯⎯⎯⎯⎯⎯⎯⎯⎯⎯Title/Position ⎯⎯⎯⎯⎯⎯⎯⎯⎯⎯⎯⎯Date⎯⎯⎯⎯⎯

⎯⎯⎯⎯⎯⎯⎯⎯⎯⎯⎯⎯⎯Title/Position ⎯⎯⎯⎯⎯⎯⎯⎯⎯⎯⎯⎯Date⎯⎯⎯⎯⎯

Babies Born with a Low Birthweight (weighing 5.5 pounds or less) are more likely to:

- Have learning disabilities
- Fail school
- Have health related problems
- Have overall low academic performance
- Be retained in grade
- Have a short attention span
- Have developmental delays

Note: None of the consequences associated with low birthweight are absolutes. There are always exceptions.

Appendix S

For use with questions 34, 35

Advice on School Entrance Regarding Children Born Prematurely

When considering school entrance for a child born prematurely, use the due date, **not** the actual birth date.

Example: The school cut-off date for kindergarten entrance is September 1st. The baby was due in the middle of October, but was born in late August or about six weeks premature. This child should be considered a mid-October birth for school entrance and grade/program placement purposes.

Parents are advised to consider one of the following options.

Have the child . . .
- Remain at home for an extra year *
- Spend an extra year in preschool *
- Attend a pre-kindergarten for young fives
- Spend two years in kindergarten
- Attend a pre-first grade program
- Remain three years in a two-grade multiage classroom

*These options are only available to financially advantaged parents.

Accommodation and Modification Ideas

1. Seat the student near the front of the classroom (preferential seating)

2. Use high-interest reading material at an easier level

3. Seat the student in close proximity to the teacher (fixed seat assignment)

4. Use color overlays over printed materials (this helps some children with dyslexia)

5. Require shortened/adjusted writing assignments (reduce volume)

6. Provide a desk carrel

7. Use noise-suppressing headsets

8. Seat the student away from the door or windows

9. Use talking books

10. Use 3-sided rubber pencil grips

11. Use student contracts

12. Minimize board copying

13. Provide cooperative learning opportunities

14. Change the percent of work required

15. Provide erasable ink pens

16. Use high quality white bonded paper that allows for easy erasing

17. Use highlighting tape and markers

18. Provide two sets of textbooks; one for school, and one for home

19. Reduce auditory and visual distractions

20. Provide and maintain a quiet work space

21. Provide direct instruction when appropriate

22. Use a variety of alternative assessments to evaluate student work

23. Accept oral recordings as an alternative to writing assignments

24. Provide a multiplication/division table chart

25. Provide a desktop cursive writing line

26. Allow the use of calculators when appropriate

27. Give additional time to complete tests

28. Give tests orally as necessary

29. Provide clarification of directions

30. Pre-teach new concepts

31. Give verbal and/or visual cues to increase time-on-task behavior

32. Provide multi-sensory presentations of directions

33. Provide multi-sensory presentations of lessons (auditory, kinesthetic, visual)

34. Break down multi-step directions

For use with questions 23, 24, 36

Accommodations for Alcohol/Drug-Damaged Students

These students need:

- A small, self-contained class (preferably eight-to-one student-teacher ratio)

- Instruction based on multi-sensory methods

- Realistic expectations

- Assigned to a multiyear placement when appropriate (a looping or multiage classroom)

- Placement in a mixed-ability heterogeneous class

- A "fixed-seat" assignment

- A "rigid" classroom routine with clear, consistent rules and guidelines

- Protection from loud noise

- Peer and cross-age tutoring opportunities

- Increased time spent on a single topic or subject

- Positive reinforcement

- Individual instruction as much as possible

- Protection from disturbing visual stimulation

- Quiet space opportunities

- Technology/media-assisted instruction

- Schedule which matches their strongest period of the day with major academic subjects

- A minimal amount of change

- Placement with a teacher who is:
  - Patient
  - Predictable
  - Tolerant
  - Trustworthy
  - Kind/understanding
  - A firm disciplinarian

Appendix V

CONFIDENTIAL

THE
Retention/
Promotion
CHECKLIST

Traits of a Student with Behavior Problems

Please check all traits that apply to: _____ Date _____
Student's name

Caution: Do not use this information to identify, diagnose or label any student as behaviorally disturbed. This information is for discussion purposes only. A diagnosis of a behavioral disorder should only be made by a psychologist in conjunction with a pediatrician or family doctor.

How often have you observed this student exhibiting the following traits:	Often	Sometimes	Rarely	Never
Argumentative behavior				
Defies adult authority				
Displays unprovoked aggression or violence toward others				
Uses inappropriate language				
Lacks self-control				
Exhibits impulsive behavior				
Demonstrates difficulty getting along socially with peers				
Takes things that don't belong to him/her				
Exhibits disruptive behavior				
Is deliberately excluded from social interaction by other students				
Has difficulty doing the right thing				
Seems unable to understand the limits of acceptable behavior				

Note: Many students display a few traits of behavior problems at times. Serious concern is warranted when a student exhibits multiple traits over an extended period of time. If the "often" is checked repeatedly, then this student should be referred to the school guidance counselor for services. It is also recommended that this student be placed with a teacher who is patient, tolerant, kind/understanding, predictable, a firm disciplinarian, and has been trained to work with students with special problems.

Certain personal characteristics or traits may also be indicative of other problems or conditions such as: depression, school-related stress, social difficulty, emotional difficulty, learning disabilities, as well as Attention Deficit Disorder. None of these traits of behavior problems are absolutes.

Name(s) of the individual(s) who provided this information:

_____Title/Position _____Date_____

_____Title/Position _____Date_____

For use with question 40, 41, 42

Traits of the Difficult Child

Please check all traits that apply to: _____ Date_____

Student's name

Caution: Do not use this information to identify, diagnose or label any student as a difficult child. The use of this information should be strictly for discussion purposes.

How often have you observed this student exhibiting the following traits:	Often	Sometimes	Rarely	Never
Whines and complains about things in general				
Tends to pout				
Demonstrates difficulty following school rules				
Exhibits aggressive/disruptive behavior				
Tends to be insensitive to verbal and nonverbal social cues				
Has difficulty adapting to change				
Seems dissatisfied with life				
Is easily disappointed				
Tends to be noncompliant				
Takes an uncompromising stance (is stubborn)				
Tends to be intense and react strongly to most everything and everyone				

Note: Many students can be difficult at times. Serious concern is warranted when a student displays multiple traits of being difficult over an extended period of time. Certain characteristics or traits may also be indicative of other problems or conditions such as: emotional difficulty, social difficulty and/or behavior problems.

Name of the individual(s) who provided this information:

_____Title/Position _____Date_____

_____Title/Position _____Date_____

Auditing Your Retention/Promotion Policy

This audit will help you evaluate your current retention/promotion practices and create a policy that is effective, beneficial for children, and ethically and legally defensible. A model policy addresses the following factors, circumstances and practices.

Please check the boxes that indicate your current policy or practices.

Characteristics of a Comprehensive Retention/Promotion Policy	True for our school system	Not true at this time for our school system
1. While the placement of students is the legal prerogative of the superintendent of schools, retention/promotion decisions are mutually agreeable to both school officials and the parent(s)/guardian(s).		
2. Retention/promotion decisions are made based on the recommendations of an ad hoc child study team that includes:		
A. The principal		
B. The teacher(s)		
C. Parent(s) and/or guardian(s)		
And may include:		
D. A counselor		
E. Learning specialist(s)		
F. Social worker(s)		
G. A psychologist		
H. Other: _____		
3. When appropriate, the child study team creates and implements an Individual Retention Plan (IRP) or Individual Promotion Plan (IPP)		
4. Retention/promotion decisions consider the following factors or circumstances:		
A. Academic attainment/needs		
B. Social maturity		
C. Emotional maturity		
D. Physical size/development		
E. Ability level		
F. Primary language		
G. Learning disabilities		
H. Gender		
I. Attendance		

	True for our school system	Not true at this time for our school system
J. Transiency		
K. ESL		
L. Student motivation		
M. Chronological age		
N. Student attitude		
O. Parent support		
P. Overall health and wellbeing (vision, hearing, physical disability, malnutrition, chemical damage, trauma, poverty)		
Q. Other: _____		
5. A retention decision is never based on a single indicator such as reading level or standardized achievement tests.		
6. When possible, retention takes place in the early years (pre-school through grade three)		
7. Retention of students after grade three is approached with extreme caution.		
8. Retained students are given additional support services when needed. (Without appropriate services the positive impact of retention is substantially reduced.)		
9. A student is not placed in a grade where he or she is more than 1 year older than his/her classmates.		
10. Students are not given an additional "extra year of learning time" if they:		
A. Stayed home an extra year		
B. Have already been retained in grade		
C. Spent an extra year in a day care or preschool setting		
D. Remained an extra year in a multiage classroom		
E. Took an extra year in a transition grade/program		
11. Retention is not used:		
A. As a punishment		
B. To motivate a student academically		
C. In place of special education services		
D. To "red shirt" a student for athletic or academic purposes		
E. To address transiency-related problems		
F. To supplant remedial instruction		
G. In place of ESL services		
H. To compensate for excessive absenteeism (15 or more days per school year)		

Individual Retention Plan (IRP)

Individual Promotion Plan (IPP)

Individual Retention Plan (IRP)

Student _____ Date of Birth _____
(Name)

Present grade placement _____ Date _____

Placement Recommendation (grade level/program) _____

School _____ Phone _____

Parent(s)/Guardian(s) _____
Name(s)

Mailing Address _____ Phone _____

Child Study Team Manager _____ Title/Role _____

Principal _____
Name

Classroom Teacher(s) _____
Name(s)

Parent(s)/Guardian(s) Approval   ☐   I/we approve this IRP

   ☐   I/we do not approve this IRP

Parent(s)/Guardian(s) Signature_____ Date _____

Parent(s)/Guardian(s) Signature_____ Date _____

The undersigned individuals participated in the writing of this IRP

Name	Title/Role	Date
_____	_____	_____
_____	_____	_____
_____	_____	_____
_____	_____	_____
_____	_____	_____
_____	_____	_____

Student _____ Date _____

Additional Intervention Programs and Services (IRP)

Goal: _____

_____

Intervention/Services: _____

_____

_____

_____

_____

_____

Implemented by: _____

Title/Role: _____

Progress Review

Date: _____

Comments: _____

_____

_____

_____

_____

_____

_____

_____

Goal: _____

_____

Intervention/Services: _____

_____

_____

_____

_____

_____

Implemented by: _____

Title/Role: _____

Progress Review

Date: _____

Comments: _____

_____

_____

_____

_____

_____

_____

_____

Goal: _____

_____

Intervention/Services: _____

_____

_____

_____

_____

_____

Implemented by: _____

Title/Role: _____

Progress Review

Date: _____

Comments: _____

_____

_____

_____

_____

_____

_____

_____

Student _____ Date_____

Instructional Accommodations (IRP)

Goal: _____

_____

Accommodations: _____

_____

_____

_____

_____

_____

Implemented by: _____

Title/Role: _____

Progress Review

Date: _____

Comments: _____

_____

_____

_____

_____

_____

_____

_____

Goal: _____

_____

Accommodations: _____

_____

_____

_____

_____

_____

Implemented by: _____

Title/Role: _____

Progress Review

Date: _____

Comments: _____

_____

_____

_____

_____

_____

_____

Goal: _____

_____

Accommodations: _____

_____

_____

_____

_____

_____

Implemented by: _____

Title/Role: _____

Progress Review

Date: _____

Comments: _____

_____

_____

_____

_____

_____

_____

Student _____ Date _____

Curriculum Modifications (IRP)

Goal: _____
_____

Modifications: _____
_____
_____
_____
_____
_____
_____

Implemented by: _____

Title/Role: _____

Progress Review

Date: _____

Comments: _____
_____
_____
_____
_____
_____
_____
_____

Goal: _____
_____

Modifications: _____
_____
_____
_____
_____
_____
_____

Implemented by: _____

Title/Role: _____

Progress Review

Date: _____

Comments: _____
_____
_____
_____
_____
_____
_____
_____

Goal: _____
_____

Modifications: _____
_____
_____
_____
_____
_____
_____

Implemented by: _____

Title/Role: _____

Progress Review

Date: _____

Comments: _____
_____
_____
_____
_____
_____
_____
_____

Individual Promotion Plan (IPP)

Student _____ Date of Birth _____
(Name)

Present Grade Placement _____ Date _____

Placement Recommendation (grade level/program) _____

School _____ Phone _____

Parent(s)/Guardian(s) _____
Name(s)

Mailing Address _____ Phone _____

Child Study Team Manager _____ Title/Role _____

Principal _____
Name

Classroom Teacher(s) _____
Name(s)

Parent(s)/Guardian(s) Approval ☐ I/we approve this IPP

☐ I/we do not approve this IPP

Parent(s)/Guardian(s) Signature_____ Date _____

Parent(s)/Guardian(s) Signature_____ Date _____

The undersigned individuals participated in the writing of this IPP

Name	Title/Role	Date
_____	_____	_____
_____	_____	_____
_____	_____	_____
_____	_____	_____
_____	_____	_____
_____	_____	_____

Student _____ Date _____

Additional Intervention Programs and Services (IPP)

Goal: _____

_____

Intervention/Services: _____

_____

_____

_____

_____

_____

Implemented by: _____

Title/Role: _____

Progress Review

Date: _____

Comments: _____

_____

_____

_____

_____

_____

_____

_____

Goal: _____

_____

Intervention/Services: _____

_____

_____

_____

_____

_____

Implemented by: _____

Title/Role: _____

Progress Review

Date: _____

Comments: _____

_____

_____

_____

_____

_____

_____

_____

Goal: _____

_____

Intervention/Services: _____

_____

_____

_____

_____

_____

Implemented by: _____

Title/Role: _____

Progress Review

Date: _____

Comments: _____

_____

_____

_____

_____

_____

_____

_____

Student _____ Date _____

Instructional Accommodations (IPP)

Goal: _____
_____

Accommodations: _____
_____
_____
_____
_____
_____

Implemented by: _____

Title/Role: _____

Progress Review

Date: _____

Comments: _____
_____
_____
_____
_____
_____
_____
_____

Goal: _____
_____

Accommodations: _____
_____
_____
_____
_____
_____

Implemented by: _____

Title/Role: _____

Progress Review

Date: _____

Comments: _____
_____
_____
_____
_____
_____
_____
_____

Goal: _____
_____

Accommodations: _____
_____
_____
_____
_____
_____

Implemented by: _____

Title/Role: _____

Progress Review

Date: _____

Comments: _____
_____
_____
_____
_____
_____
_____
_____

Student _____ Date: _____

Curriculum Modifications (IPP)

Goal: _____
_____

Modifications: _____
_____
_____
_____
_____
_____

Implemented by: _____

Title/Role: _____

Progress Review

Date: _____

Comments: _____
_____
_____
_____
_____
_____
_____
_____

Goal: _____
_____

Modifications: _____
_____
_____
_____
_____
_____

Implemented by: _____

Title/Role: _____

Progress Review

Date: _____

Comments: _____
_____
_____
_____
_____
_____
_____
_____

Goal: _____
_____

Modifications: _____
_____
_____
_____
_____
_____

Implemented by: _____

Title/Role: _____

Progress Review

Date: _____

Comments: _____
_____
_____
_____
_____
_____
_____

Samples of Completed Checklists and Individual Retention and Promotion Plans

Dear Readers,

Too often educators search for an "either/or" answer to difficult school-related problems. One such issue is that of retention and social promotion. No one we know is "for" either of these options. What is needed is an informed decision-making process, where a recommendation is made for each student, based on his/her individual circumstances.

To better understand how the retention-promotion decision-making process works for individual students, examine the two profiles that follow. The students, Mark Hayden and Lisa Nguyen, were identified by their teachers as being at risk for failure at the next grade. Their profiles were presented to a school/child study team, where a decision was made to use the Retention/Promotion Checklist to collect and analyze family and school observations.

Using the information on the checklist, a comprehensive overview of each student emerged for the team to analyze. In this final step, the risks and benefits of either retaining or promoting the student were listed, then carefully considered by the team.

Consensus on the best possible recommendation for each student was reached based on the student's individual circumstances. It was not the number of pros or cons that influenced the decision, but rather the importance of each factor, especially the student's and family's attitude about the options.

When the team met to make a summary recommendation, they decided whether or not to write an Individual Retention Plan (IRP) or an Individual Promotion Plan (IPP) for the student. The plans ensure that support will be provided, no matter what the decision.

The best way to learn how the process works is to review the pages in Mark's and Lisa's samples. These models should help you learn how to implement the decision-making process for retention or promotion.

Sincerely,

Jim Grant

Irv Richardson

The Retention/Promotion Checklist

Student _Mark Hoyden_   Date of birth _8/30/91_ Present grade placement _First grade_

Name of person responsible for completing this checklist _Emilie Bell_   Date _____

Child study team leader _Susan Scott_   Title _Principal_

Parent(s)/Guardian(s) _____ Date _____

Directions: Where indicated, please list the name of the individual(s) who provided specific information. Please pass over any items that either you or the parents/guardians are uncomfortable answering.

1. What is your best estimate of this student's potential?

   ☐ High potential   ☑ Average potential
   ☐ Above-average potential   ☐ Below average potential
   ☐ Limited potential

2. Do you or the parents/guardians suspect that this student may be a "slower learner" (70-89 IQ range)?

   ☐ Yes   ☑ No   ☐ Unsure

3. Has this student's ability been evaluated with an individually administered IQ test?

   ☐ Yes   ☑ No

   If yes, what were the findings?_____
   _____
   _____
   _____
   _____

   Name of the individual(s) who provided this information:
   Emilie Bell   Date _4/20/98_
   _____ Date _____

4. What is this student's basic academic skill level?

   ☐ Grade level   ☑ Below grade level   ☐ Unsure
   ☐ Well below grade level

   Please describe any areas of difficulty: _Mark is ½ year below grade level in reading and is at the Primer level. He has only mastered sums through six._

5. Does this student make a consistent effort to do his/her work?

   ☐ Always   ☑ Most of the time   ☐ Sometimes
   ☐ Seldom   ☐ Never

   Comments: _He completes his work in the morning but is unable to finish his work in the afternoon._
   _____
   _____

6. How would you describe this student's level of motivation?

   ☐ High motivation   ☑ Average motivation
   ☐ Low motivation

   Comments: _He is motivated when he does activities that interest him._
   _____
   _____
   _____

7a. Has this student been identified as learning disabled?

   ☐ Yes   ☑ No

   If yes, what is the nature of the disability?_____
   _____
   _____
   _____
   _____

7b. If the answer to question number 7a was "No," do you or the parents/guardians suspect that this student may have some type of unidentified learning problem?

☐ Yes ☐ No ☑ Unsure at this time

If yes or unsure at this time, please comment: _____

_____

_____

_____

_____

Name of the individual(s) who provided this information:

Emilie Bell Date 4/20/98

_____ Date _____

8. Do you or the parents/guardians have concerns about this student's ability to meet grade-level standards if the student is promoted to the next grade?

☑ Yes ☐ No

If yes, please comment: _____

_____

_____

_____

_____

Name of the individual(s) who provided this information:

Emilie Bell Date 4/20/98

_____ Date _____

9. This student is a: ☑ Boy ☐ Girl

10. Has this student ever skipped a grade?

☐ Yes ☑ No

If yes, please indicate the grade level skipped. _____

11. Was this student an early school entrant (entered school underage)?

☐ Yes ☑ No

12. What was this student's chronological age at the time of school entrance? __6__ years __0__ months

13a. Do you or the parents/guardians think this student's behavior is developmentally young for his/her chronological age in relation to same-age peers?

☑ Yes ☐ No ☐ Unsure at this time

If yes or unsure at this time, please comment: _____

He seems extremely immature for his age

_____

_____

13b. Do you or the parents/guardians think this student's behavior is developmentally young for his/her present grade-level placement in relation to same-age peers?

☑ Yes ☐ No ☐ Unsure at this time

If yes or unsure at this time, please comment: _____

He seems overall too young for his first grade placement.

_____

Name of the individual(s) who provided this information:

Emilie Bell Date 4/20/98

_____ Date _____

14. In your opinion, is this student assigned to the wrong grade?

☑ Yes ☐ No ☐ Unsure at this time

If yes, or unsure at this time, please comment: __He__ constantly asked to visit the kindergarten. He is a very immature first grader. He cries whenever a new concept is introduced.

_____

15. Has this student ever had an extra year of learning time in any form?

☐ Yes   ☑ No

If yes, please indicate if this student:

☐ Stayed home an extra year

☐ Spent an extra year in a day care or preschool setting

☐ Took an extra year in a transition grade/program (i.e. pre-kindergarten, pre-first, pre-second, pre-third)

☐ Has already been retained in grade

☐ Remained an extra year in a multiage classroom

☐ Other (please specify) _____

Name of the individual(s) who provided this information:

Emilie Bell ___ Date _4/20/98_

_____ Date _____

STOP - If this student has already had an additional year of learning time, retention is not an appropriate intervention. This child should be promoted and given support services, see questions 22-24 and refer to the Individual Promotion Plan (IPP).

16. Does this student exhibit signs and signals of school-related stress?

☑ Yes   ☐ No

If yes, check all stress signs and signals that apply:

At home – How often does this student:

	Often	Sometimes	Rarely	Never
A.) Revert to bedwetting?	☐	☐	☐	☑
B.) Not want to go to school?	☑	☐	☐	☐
C.) Suffer from stomachaches or headaches, particularly in the morning before school?	☑	☐	☐	☐
D.) Dislike school or complain that school is "dumb"?	☑	☐	☐	☐

If some of the areas checked were under "Often," please comment: _Mark says school is stupid and often says, "I hate school". He often asks to stay home._

_____

_____

Name of the individual(s) who provided information on Section A-D: _Marjorie Hayden_ Date _4/20/98_

_____ Date _____

At school – How often does this student:

	Often	Sometimes	Rarely	Never
E.) Want to play with younger children?	☑	☐	☐	☐
F.) Miss school?	☐	☑	☐	☐
G.) Complain about being bored with schoolwork, when in reality he/she cannot do the work?	☑	☐	☐	☐
H.) Have difficulty paying attention or staying on task?	☑	☐	☐	☐
I.) Have difficulty following the daily routine?	☑	☐	☐	☐
J.) Seem unable to shift easily from one task to the next, one adult to the next, one situation to the next?	☐	☑	☐	☐

If some of the areas checked were under "Often," please comment: _Mark likes playing with kindergarten students. He has difficulty paying attention and staying on task. His school work is inconsistent._

_____

Name of the individual(s) who provided information on Section E-J:

Emilie Bell ___ Date _4/20/98_

_____ Date _____

In General – How often does this student:

	Often	Sometimes	Rarely	Never
K.) Become withdrawn?	☐	☑	☐	☐
L.) Complain that he/she has no friends?	☐	☑	☐	☐
M.) Cry easily and frequently?	☑	☐	☐	☐
N.) Seem depressed?	☐	☑	☐	☐
O.) Tire quickly?	☐	☐	☐	☑
P.) Need constant reassurance and praise?	☐	☑	☐	☐
Q.) Act harried/hurried?	☑	☐	☐	☐
R.) Show signs of a nervous tic (i.e., frequent clearing of the throat, pulling out hair, twitching eye, nervous cough)?	☐	☐	☐	☑

If some of the areas checked were under "Often," please comment: _He cries frequently when he is frustrated with his school work. He seems stressed and anxious much of the time._

Name of the individual(s) who provided information on Section K-R:

Emilie Bell Date _4/20/98_

Marjorie Hayden Date _4/20/98_

(Note: All children display some kind of stress at times. Severe stress is indicated when a child consistently displays several stress signs over an extended period of time.)

17a. What is this student's attendance record?

☑ Good attendance ☐ High absenteeism (15 or more days per year)

This student was absent _____ out of _____ school days.

17b. If this student has had high absenteeism, was it due to illness or disability?

☐ Yes ☑ No

If yes, please comment: _____

18. Is this student's family highly transient (moved three or more times in five years)?

☐ Yes ☑ No

If yes, how often has the family moved since this student started school? _____

Student's History of School Difficulty

19. Has this student experienced serious difficulty in any of the following grades/programs? Please check all that apply. (N/A = Not applicable)

	Yes	No	N/A
Day Care	☐	☐	☑
Preschool/PreK	☑	☐	☐
Head Start	☐	☐	☑
*Pre-kindergarten	☐	☐	☑
Kindergarten	☑	☐	☐
*Pre-first	☐	☐	☑
First Grade	☑	☐	☐
*Pre-second	☐	☐	☐
Second Grade	☐	☐	☐
*Pre-third	☐	☐	☐
Third Grade	☐	☐	☐
Fourth Grade	☐	☐	☐
Fifth Grade	☐	☐	☐
Sixth Grade	☐	☐	☐

* Transition Grades/Programs

Other _____

If yes to any of the above, please comment: _We withdrew him from preschool because he cried constantly. Last year's teacher felt Mark would benefit from another year in kindergarten_

Name of the individual(s) who provided this information:

Marjorie Hayden Date _4/20/98_

_____ Date _____

20. Does this student speak English as a second language or have limited English proficiency?

☐ Yes ☑ No

If yes, does or has this student received ESL/LEP support services?

☐ Yes ☐ No

21a. Do you or the parents/guardians have reason to believe this student has a poor self-concept?

☑ Yes ☐ No ☐ Unsure at this time

If yes or unsure at this time, please comment: _____

Mark crawls under his desk and cries. He says he can't do his work. Mark tends to be easily discouraged.

21b. If the answer was "Yes" or "unsure at this time" to question number 21a, do you or the parents/guardians believe this student's poor self-concept is directly related to the student's school difficulty?

☑ Yes ☐ No ☐ Unsure at this time

If yes or unsure at this time, please comment: _____

Mother does not see the crying at home. Seems to only happen at school.

Name of the individual(s) who provided this information:

Emilie Bell Date 4/20/98

Marjorie Hayden Date 4/20/98

22. Check all intervention programs and services that have been tried with this student to date:

☐ Accelerated learning ☑ Remediation
☐ Counseling ☑ Summer school(s)
☐ Special education ☑ Title I support
☐ Private tutoring ☐ In-school tutoring
☐ ESL/LEP ☐ Speech/language support services

☐ Other _____
☐ Other _____

Please comment on the results of these interventions/programs and services: He is receiving Reading Recovery and is making excellent gains. Mark meets with the counselor once a week in a small group. Group activities focus on building confidence. Mrs. Hayden has a private tutor to work with Mark on reading.

23. What classroom accommodations and modifications have been made to date? Mark sits next to the teacher. His desk has a carrel to reduce distractions. His work load has been reduced

Please comment on the results of these classroom adaptations. He likes being near the teacher to get extra help. Mark likes the privacy he gets with his desk carrel. He goes readily to the counseling sessions.

24. Please list additional interventions programs and services that will be provided for this student next year: Mark will continue receiving additional reading support until he has reached grade level.

Health/Well-Being
(Optional Questions)

Questions 25-43 cover what may be considered private family matters. Due to the extremely sensitive nature of these questions confidentiality must be protected. Information provided by parents/guardians should only be available to the child study team. **Parents/guardians are not required to answer any of these questions.**

25a. Is this student's physical development within the normal range for his/her age as determined by a physician?

☐ Yes　☑ No

If no, please comment: _Mark has always been small physically for his age_

25b. Do you or the parents/guardians think this student is physically: (check one)

☐ Average size for his/her age?
☑ Small for his/her age?
☐ Large for his/her age?

Comments: _He is among the smallest boys in my class._

Name of the individual(s) who provided this information:
Emillie Bell Date _4/20/98_

_____ Date _____

26. Does this student have serious medical problems, such as:

Diabetes?　☐ Yes　☑ No
Asthma?　☐ Yes　☑ No
Allergies?　☐ Yes　☑ No

Other? (please specify) _____

If yes to any of the above, please comment: _____

_____
_____
_____
_____

Name of the individual(s) who provided this information:
Marjorie Hayden Date _4/20/98_

_____ Date _____

27. Has this student had any serious childhood illnesses such as:

Encephalitis?　☐ Yes　☑ No
Spinal meningitis?　☐ Yes　☑ No
Whooping cough?　☐ Yes　☑ No

Other? (please specify) _____

If yes to any of the above, please comment: _____

_____
_____
_____
_____
_____
_____

Name of the individual(s) who provided this information:
Marjorie Hayden Date _4/20/98_

_____ Date _____

28. Has this student ever suffered a serious childhood accident?

☐ Yes　☑ No

If yes, please comment: _____

_____
_____
_____
_____
_____

Name of the individual(s) who provided this information:
Marjorie Hayden Date _4/20/98_

_____ Date _____

29. Has this child ever been exposed to toxic substances such as lead, pesticides, inhalants, etc.?

☐ Yes ☑ No

If yes please comment: _____

_____

_____

_____

_____

Name of the individual(s) who provided this information:

Marjorie Hayden Date 4/20/98

_____ Date _____

30. Do you or the parents/guardians suspect this student has:

Vision problems? ☐ Yes ☑ No ☐ Unsure

Auditory problems? ☐ Yes ☐ No ☑ Unsure

If yes or unsure, please comment: We are going to have his hearing tested. He had repeated ear infections.

_____

_____

Name of the individual(s) who provided this information:

Marjorie Hayden Date 4/20/98

_____ Date _____

31. Does this student have a serious physical disability?

☐ Yes ☑ No

If yes, please comment: _____

_____

_____

_____

_____

Name of the individual(s) who provided this information:

Marjorie Hayden Date 4/20/98

_____ Date _____

32. Does this student's family live at or below the poverty level?

☐ Yes ☑ No

If yes, please comment: _____

_____

_____

_____

_____

Name of the individual(s) who provided this information:

Marjorie Hayden Date 4/20/98

_____ Date _____

33. Was this child's birth considered traumatic/difficult?

☐ Yes ☑ No

If yes, please comment: _____

_____

_____

_____

_____

Name of the individual(s) who provided this information:

Marjorie Hayden Date 4/20/98

_____ Date _____

34. Was this child born with a low birth weight?

☑ Yes ☐ No

If yes, please check:

☑ Low birth weight (5.5 lbs. or less)

☐ Very low birth weight (approximately 3.5 lbs. or less)

Comments: When he was born he weighed 5 lbs. 6 oz. He was slow to creep, walk, talk and toilet train.

Name of the individual(s) who provided this information:

Marjorie Hayden Date 4/20/98

_____ Date _____

35. Was this child born premature?

☑ Yes ☐ No

If yes, please check:

☑ Premature

☐ Extremely premature (approximately 25 weeks or less)

Comments: *He was born 3 weeks premature. He was due September 20, 1991.*

Name of the individual(s) who provided this information:

Marjorie Hayden Date 4/20/98

_____ Date _____

36. During the pregnancy, was the mother:
(check all that apply)

A. ☐ Abusing drugs/alcohol?

B. ☐ Smoking/exposed to secondhand smoke?

C. ☐ Malnourished?

D. ☐ Exposed to toxic substances (i.e., lead, pesticides, inhalants, etc.)?

E. ☐ Experiencing extreme stress (i.e., traumatized by divorce, abuse, poverty, etc.)?

F. ☐ Other (please specify): _____

Please comment on any factors or circumstances checked: _____

N/A

Name of the individual(s) who provided this information:

_____ Date _____

_____ Date _____

37. Has this child ever suffered from malnutrition?

☐ Yes ☑ No

If yes, please comment: _____

_____

_____

_____

_____

Name of the individual(s) who provided this information:

Marjorie Hayden Date 4/20/98

_____ Date _____

38. Has this child had a traumatic experience such as:

Someone close to the child has died?

☑ Yes ☐ No

The child has witnessed or has been the victim of a violent act?

☐ Yes ☑ No

The child's family was or is in crisis?
(For example, going through a divorce)

☐ Yes ☑ No

Moving to a new home?

☐ Yes ☑ No

Someone close to the child was (or is) terminally ill or injured?

☑ Yes ☐ No

Other (please specify) _____

If yes to any of the above, please comment: *His grandmother lived with us. She was sick for 2 years and passed away when he was 4½ years old. This was a very difficult time for Mark.*

Name of the individual(s) who provided this information:

Marjorie Hayden Date 4/20/98

_____ Date _____

39a. Do you or the parents/guardians suspect this child may be suffering from depression?

☐ Yes ☐ No ☑ Unsure at this time

If unsure at this time, please comment: _Mark Cries Frequently at school but not at home._

39b. If the answer to question number 39a was "Yes," what signs of depression does this child display?

Often seems sad	☐ Yes	☑ No
Does not seem to have fun or enjoy school	☑ Yes	☐ No
Does not want to participate in activities	☑ Yes	☐ No
Prefers to be alone	☐ Yes	☑ No
Lacks enthusiasm	☐ Yes	☑ No

Please comment: _Mark resists participating in activities involving seat work_

Name of the individual(s) who provided this information:
Emilie Bell Date _4/20/98_
_____ Date _____

40. Have you or the parents/guardians noticed this student displaying any signs of emotional problems such as:

Frequent, uncontrollable outbursts?	☑ Yes	☐ No
Withdrawn, unable to relate to others?	☑ Yes	☐ No
Frequent lying to parents/guardians?	☐ Yes	☑ No

Other? _____

If yes, please comment: _Mark has temper tantrums when he is frustrated. He prefers playing with younger children when given the chance._

Name of the individual(s) who provided this information:
Emilie Bell Date _4/20/98_ .
Marjorie Hayden Date _4/20/98_

41. Do you or the parents/guardians think this student exhibits any serious behavior problems such as:

Frequent defiance of adults?	☐ Yes	☑ No
Aggressive/violent behavior towards others?	☐ Yes	☑ No
Frequent use of inappropriate language?	☐ Yes	☑ No

Other? (please specify) _____

If yes, please comment: _He is a very well mannered child_

Name of the individual(s) who provided this information:
Emilie Bell Date _4/20/98_
Marjorie Hayden Date _4/20/98_

42. Do you or the parents/guardians feel this student exhibits signs of social problems such as:

Being unable to make or keep friends?	☑ Yes	☐ No
Does not get along with his/her peer group?	☑ Yes	☐ No
Has difficulty sharing/taking turns?	☐ Yes	☑ No
Tends to say or do inappropriate things?	☐ Yes	☑ No

If yes, please comment: _He prefers to play with younger children. He has difficulty relating to his classmates._

Name of the individual(s) who provided this information:
Emilie Bell Date _4/20/98_
_____ Date _____

43. What other issues should the child study team consider (siblings, is this a foster child, etc.)? _____

_____

N/A

_____

_____

End of Optional Health/Well-Being Questions

44. What is this student's attitude toward remaining at the same grade level an additional year?

Student supports staying at the same grade level for an additional year.

[✓] Yes   [ ] No   [ ] Unsure at this time

Student is opposed to staying at the same grade level for an additional year.

[ ] Yes   [✓] No   [ ] Unsure at this time

Comments: _Mark seemed almost relieved at the prospect of spending another year in first grade._

45. What is this student's attitude toward being promoted to the next grade?

Student supports being promoted to the next grade.

[ ] Yes   [✓] No   [ ] Unsure at this time

Student is opposed to being promoted to the next grade.

[✓] Yes   [ ] No   [ ] Unsure at this time

Comments: _Mark is nervous about being a second grader._

46. How do the parents/guardians feel about having their child remain at the same grade level for an additional year?

[✓] They support their child remaining at the same grade level an additional year.

[ ] They are unsure at this time about having their child remain at the same grade level an additional year.

[ ] They are opposed to having their child remain at the same grade level an additional year.

Comments: _We wanted Mark to repeat kindergarten, but the previous principal didn't support us. We would like Mark to repeat 1st grade_

Name of the individual(s) who provided this information:
Marjorie Hayden Date _4/20/98_
_____ Date _____

47. How do the parents/guardians feel about their child being promoted?

[ ] They support their child being promoted to the next grade.

[ ] They are unsure at this time about having their child being promoted to the next grade.

[✓] They are opposed to having their child being promoted to the next grade.

Comments: _____

_____

_____

_____

_____

_____

_____

Name of the individual(s) who provided this information:
Marjorie Hayden Date _4/20/98_
_____ Date _____

48. The child study team members believe that this student should be:

☐ Promoted ☑ Retained ☐ Unsure at this time
Principal _Susan Scott_

☐ Promoted ☑ Retained ☐ Unsure at this time
Teacher(s) _Emilie Bell_

☐ Promoted ☑ Retained ☐ Unsure at this time
School counselor _Willa Cole_

☐ Promoted ☑ Retained ☐ Unsure at this time
School psychologist _John Wilmer_

☐ Promoted ☐ Retained ☐ Unsure at this time
Learning specialist _____

☐ Promoted ☑ Retained ☐ Unsure at this time
Child study team leader _Susan Scott_

☐ Promoted ☐ Retained ☐ Unsure at this time
Other _____

☐ Promoted ☐ Retained ☐ Unsure at this time
Other _____

☐ Promoted ☐ Retained ☐ Unsure at this time
Other _____

Comments: _____
_____
_____

RECOMMENDATION

49. The child study team recommends that this student:

A. ☐ Be promoted to the next grade level and receive support services such as remediation, accelerated learning, summer school, etc.

B. ☐ Be promoted to the next grade level and stay with the same teacher in a looping configuration.

C. ☐ Be placed in a transition grade/program (i.e., pre-kindergarten, pre-first, pre-second, pre-third).

D. ☐ Remain another year at the same grade level with the same teacher.

E. ☐ Remain another year at the same grade level, but with a different teacher.

F. ☐ Remain another year at the same grade level, but in a different school setting. (This option may not be possible in some school systems.)

G. ☒ Remain an additional year in a multiage classroom.

H. ☐ Be re-placed back one grade level mid-year.

I. ☐ Other (please specify): _____
_____
_____

Comments: _____
_____
_____
_____
_____
_____
_____

50. The child study team is encouraged to create and implement either an Individual Retention Plan (IRP) or Individual Promotion Plan (IPP) for this student. This good faith plan is a non-binding, non-legal agreement created by the child study team focusing on identified goals to ensure school success for this student. This individual plan outlines a course of action that specifies what intervention programs, services and adaptations will be implemented, who will take responsibility to see that it happens as well as when they will happen. **The child study team recommends an:**

☒ Individual Retention Plan ☐ Individual Promotion Plan ☐ IRP/IPP is not necessary at this time
If a plan is to be created and implemented, who will be the child study team person responsible for managing the plan?

Susan Scott   _Principal_
Name   Title/Role

The child study team will meet again on _Sept. 21_ **to follow up on this student's progress.**

Retention / Promotion Checklist:
Summary & Recommendations

> The following summary is based on information and observations from the checklist, as documented by parents/guardians and school personnel.
>
> The school believes student placement decisions should be made on an informed, individual basis.
>
> Any decision will have pros and cons for the student. These factors are weighed out to make a placement recommendation that is in the best interest of the individual student. Along with the placement recommendation, an Individual Retention Plan (IRP) or an Individual Promotion Plan (IPP) is included where appropriate. The IRP or IPP is a plan of action for each student that includes program interventions and services, including instructional accommodations and curriculum modifications.

Student Name: **Mark Hayden**   Date: **4/27/98**   School Year: **1998-99**

Placement Recommendation: (see attached summary)

[✓] **Retention**   **Individual Retention Plan**   (Yes)   No

[ ] **Promotion**   **Individual Promotion Plan**   Yes   No

Next year's teacher: **Linda Holden's 1-2 Multiage Classroom**

Summary prepared by: **Susan Scott and Emilie Bell**

I/We accept/reject this recommendation:

Marjorie Hayden   _April 29, 1998_
Signature of parent/guardian   Date

_____   _____
Signature of parent/guardian   Date

Retention/ Promotion Checklist:
Summary & Recommendations For

Mark Hayden

Student's Name

PROS	CONS
1. Mark has expressed relief when asked about spending another year in first grade.	1. Reading Recovery will not be available.
2. He has not had an extra year of school.	2. Mark will not move ahead with his peers.
3. He is small in size for his age.	3. He will not be with the same teacher.
4. He is young for his age — he chooses to play with children in the kindergarten class.	
5. He often asks to work in the kindergarten room.	
6. At home, he frequently says that school is dumb.	
7. His individual intelligence screening reflects at least average ability at this time.	
8. Since preschool, Mark has demonstrated multiple recurring stress signs.	
9. The parents support the school's recommendation.	
10. Mark's issues reflect the need to boost his confidence and help him have a positive attitude toward school.	

Comments: The team believes Mark will do well in the 1-2 multiage class. His own positive

attitude about spending another year in first grade is important to this decision.

Individual Retention Plan (IRP)

Student __Mark Hayden__ Date of Birth __8/30/91__
(Name)

Present grade placement __First grade__ Date __4/27/98__

Placement Recommendation (grade level/program) __1/2 multiage classroom__

School __Central School__ Phone __474-7918__

Parent(s)/Guardian(s) __Marjorie Hayden__
(Name(s))

Mailing Address __54 Oak Street__ Phone __474-4952__

Child Study Team Manager __Susan Scott__ Title/Role __Principal__

Principal __Susan Scott__
(Name)

Classroom Teacher(s) __Emilie Bell__
(Name(s))

Parent(s)/Guardian(s) Approval ☒ I/we approve this IRP

☐ I/we do not approve this IRP

Parent(s)/Guardian(s) Signature __Marjorie Hayden__ Date __4/27/98__

Parent(s)/Guardian(s) Signature _____ Date _____

The undersigned individuals participated in the writing of this IRP

Name	Title/Role	Date
Susan Scott	Principal/Child Study Team Manager	4-27-98
Emilie Bell	1st grade teacher	4/27/98
Willa Cole	Counselor	4-27-98
John Wilmer	School psychologist	4-27-98

Student _Mark Hayden_   Date _4/27/98_

Additional Intervention Programs and Services (IRP)

	Progress Review
Goal: To maintain reading gains and work on decoding skills Intervention/Services: Summer School. The focus of this program will be to maintain his reading gain and provide decoding skills Implemented by: Susan Scott Title/Role: principal	Date: _____ Comments: _____ _____ _____ _____ _____ _____ _____ _____
Goal: To bring Mark up to Grade level in Reading by June, 1999. Intervention/Services: Mark will Continue receiving remedial Reading services 1/2 hour per day. Implemented by: Marcus Johnson Title/Role: Reading Specialist	Date: _____ Comments: _____ _____ _____ _____ _____ _____ _____
Goal: To bring Mark up to grade level in Reading by June, 1999. Intervention/Services: alternate reading approach that emphasizes word families Implemented by: Linda Holden/Parent Volunteer Title/Role: Mark's teacher next year	Date: _____ Comments: _____ _____ _____ _____ _____ _____ _____

Student _Mark Hayden_   Date _4/27/98_

Instructional Accommodations (IRP)

Goal: To help Mark achieve reading independence	**Progress Review**
Accommodations: Mark will be provided a variety of talking books.	Date: _____
	Comments: _____
Implemented by: Marcus Jackson	
Title/Role: Reading Specialist	
Goal: To learn to work better in groups.	**Progress Review**
Accommodations: Opportunities will be created for Mark to work in cooperative and interest groups	Date: _____
	Comments: _____
Implemented by: Linda Holden	
Title/Role: Mark's Teacher next year	
Goal: _____	**Progress Review**
Accommodations: _____	Date: _____
	Comments: _____
Implemented by: _____	
Title/Role: _____	

Student **Mark Hayden**   Date **4/27/98**

Curriculum Modifications (IRP)

Goal: _____

Modifications: _____

does not need at this time.

Implemented by: _____

Title/Role: _____

Progress Review

Date: _____

Comments: _____

Goal: _____

Modifications: _____

Implemented by: _____

Title/Role: _____

Progress Review

Date: _____

Comments: _____

Goal: _____

Modifications: _____

Implemented by: _____

Title/Role: _____

Progress Review

Date: _____

Comments: _____

The Retention/Promotion Checklist

Student __Lisa Nguyen__ Date of birth __1 26 89__ Present grade placement __3rd__

Name of person responsible for completing this checklist __Michelle Boucher__ Date __4/21/98__

Child study team leader __Susan Scott__ Title __principal__

Parent(s)/Guardian(s) __Helen Nguyen__ Date __4-21-98__

Directions: Where indicated, please list the name of the individual(s) who provided specific information. Please pass over any items that either you or the parents/guardians are uncomfortable answering.

1. What is your best estimate of this student's potential?

   ☐ High potential ☐ Average potential

   ☐ Above-average potential ☒ Below average potential

   ☐ Limited potential

2. Do you or the parents/guardians suspect that this student may be a "slower learner" (70-89 IQ range)?

   ☐ Yes ☐ No ☒ Unsure

3. Has this student's ability been evaluated with an individually administered IQ test?

   ☒ Yes ☐ No

   If yes, what were the findings? __She scored low on a test administered by John Wilmer__

   Name of the individual(s) who provided this information:

   __Helen Nguyen__ Date __4-21-98__

   __John Wilmer__ Date __4.21.98__

4. What is this student's basic academic skill level?

   ☐ Grade level ☐ Below grade level ☐ Unsure

   ☒ Well below grade level

   Please describe any areas of difficulty: __Lisa is below 2nd grade level in reading and is presently at a beginning 3rd grade level in math.__

5. Does this student make a consistent effort to do his/her work?

   ☐ Always ☐ Most of the time ☒ Sometimes

   ☐ Seldom ☐ Never

   Comments: _____

6. How would you describe this student's level of motivation?

   ☐ High motivation ☐ Average motivation

   ☒ Low motivation

   Comments: __It has been difficult to motivate Lisa to complete schoolwork She seems disinterested in math and reading.__

7a. Has this student been identified as learning disabled?

   ☐ Yes ☒ No

   If yes, what is the nature of the disability? _____

7b. If the answer to question number 7a was "No," do you or the parents/guardians suspect that this student may have some type of unidentified learning problem?

☐ Yes   ☐ No   ☒ Unsure at this time

If yes or unsure at this time, please comment: Lisa seems to have a few signs typical of a learning disabled student.

_____

Name of the individual(s) who provided this information:

Helen Nguyen _____ Date 4-21-98

John Wilme _____ Date 4-21-98

8. Do you or the parents/guardians have concerns about this student's ability to meet grade-level standards if the student is promoted to the next grade?

☒ Yes   ☐ No

If yes, please comment: Lisa is one and one half years below grade level in reading. This will prevent her from passing 3rd grade standards.

Name of the individual(s) who provided this information:

Michelle Boucher _____ Date 4/21/98

Helen Nguyen _____ Date 4-21-98

9. This student is a: ☐ Boy   ☒ Girl

10. Has this student ever skipped a grade?

☐ Yes   ☒ No

If yes, please indicate the grade level skipped. _____

11. Was this student an early school entrant (entered school underage)?

☐ Yes   ☒ No

12. What was this student's chronological age at the time of school entrance? __5__ years __7__ months

13a. Do you or the parents/guardians think this student's behavior is developmentally young for his/her chronological age in relation to same-age peers?

☐ Yes   ☒ No   ☐ Unsure at this time

If yes or unsure at this time, please comment: _____

_____

_____

_____

_____

_____

13b. Do you or the parents/guardians think this student's behavior is developmentally young for his/her present grade-level placement in relation to same-age peers?

☐ Yes   ☒ No   ☐ Unsure at this time

If yes or unsure at this time, please comment: _____

_____

_____

_____

_____

Name of the individual(s) who provided this information:

Michelle Boucher _____ Date 4/21/98

Helen Nguyen _____ Date 4/21/98

14. In your opinion, is this student assigned to the wrong grade?

☐ Yes   ☐ No   ☒ Unsure at this time

If yes, or unsure at this time, please comment: She seems to be unable to do the work required of third graders.

_____

15. Has this student ever had an extra year of learning time in any form?

☐ Yes ☒ No

If yes, please indicate if this student:

☐ Stayed home an extra year

☐ Spent an extra year in a day care or preschool setting

☐ Took an extra year in a transition grade/program (i.e. pre-kindergarten, pre-first, pre-second, pre-third)

☐ Has already been retained in grade

☐ Remained an extra year in a multiage classroom

☐ Other (please specify) _____

Name of the individual(s) who provided this information:

Michelle Boucher Date 4/21/98

_____ Date _____

STOP - If this student has already had an additional year of learning time, retention is not an appropriate intervention. This child should be promoted and given support services, see questions 22-24 and refer to the Individual Promotion Plan (IPP).

16. Does this student exhibit signs and signals of school-related stress?

☒ Yes ☐ No

If yes, check all stress signs and signals that apply:

At home – How often does this student:

	Often	Sometimes	Rarely	Never
A.) Revert to bedwetting?	☐	☐	☐	☐
B.) Not want to go to school?	☒	☐	☐	☐
C.) Suffer from stomachaches or headaches, particularly in the morning before school?	☐	☒	☐	☐
D.) Dislike school or complain that school is "dumb"?	☒	☐	☐	☐

If some of the areas checked were under "Often," please comment: _Mrs. Nguyen states Lisa continues to complain that school is too hard for her and she doesn't enjoy going to school._

Name of the individual(s) who provided information on Section A-D:

Helen Nguyen Date 4-21-98

_____ Date _____

At school – How often does this student:

	Often	Sometimes	Rarely	Never
E.) Want to play with younger children?	☐	☐	☒	☐
F.) Miss school?	☒	☐	☐	☐
G.) Complain about being bored with schoolwork, when in reality he/she cannot do the work?	☒	☐	☐	☐
H.) Have difficulty paying attention or staying on task?	☒	☐	☐	☐
I.) Have difficulty following the daily routine?	☒	☐	☐	☐
J.) Seem unable to shift easily from one task to the next, one adult to the next, one situation to the next?	☒	☐	☐	☐

If some of the areas checked were under "Often," please comment: _Lisa seldom completes her assign-ments due to an in-ability to focus and stay on task._

Name of the individual(s) who provided information on Section E-J:

Michelle Boucher Date 4/21/98

_____ Date _____

In General – How often does this student:

	Often	Sometimes	Rarely	Never
K.) Become withdrawn?	☒	☐	☐	☐
L.) Complain that he/she has no friends?	☐	☐	☐	☒
M.) Cry easily and frequently?	☒	☐	☐	☐
N.) Seem depressed?	☐	☒	☐	☐
O.) Tire quickly?	☐	☐	☐	☒
P.) Need constant reassurance and praise?	☐	☐	☒	☐
Q.) Act harried/hurried?	☒	☐	☐	☐
R.) Show signs of a nervous tic (i.e., frequent clearing of the throat, pulling out hair, twitching eye, nervous cough)?	☐	☐	☐	☒

If some of the areas checked were under "Often," please comment: Lisa seems stressed and frustrated with school.

_____

_____

_____

_____

_____

_____

Name of the individual(s) who provided information on Section K-R:

Michelle Boncha Date 4/21/98

Helen Nguyen Date 4-21-98

(Note: All children display some kind of stress at times. Severe stress is indicated when a child consistently displays several stress signs over an extended period of time.)

17a. What is this student's attendance record?

☐ Good attendance ☒ High absenteeism
(15 or more days per year)

This student was absent 19 out of 150 school days.

17b. If this student has had high absenteeism, was it due to illness or disability?

☒ Yes ☐ No

If yes, please comment: Mrs. Nguyen reports Lisa misses school due to asthma.

_____

_____

_____

18. Is this student's family highly transient (moved three or more times in five years)?

☒ Yes ☐ No

If yes, how often has the family moved since this student started school? twice

Student's History of School Difficulty

19. Has this student experienced serious difficulty in any of the following grades/programs? Please check all that apply. (N/A = Not applicable)

	Yes	No	N/A
Day Care	☐	☐	☒
Preschool/PreK	☐	☐	☒
Head Start	☒	☐	☐
*Pre-kindergarten	☐	☐	☒
Kindergarten	☒	☐	☐
*Pre-first	☐	☐	☒
First Grade	☒	☐	☐
*Pre-second	☐	☐	☒
Second Grade	☒	☐	☐
*Pre-third	☐	☐	☒
Third Grade	☒	☐	☐
Fourth Grade	☐	☐	☐
Fifth Grade	☐	☐	☐
Sixth Grade	☐	☐	☐

* *Transition Grades/Programs*

Other _____

If yes to any of the above, please comment: Lisa has had a great deal of difficulty since Head Start. Lisa gets easily frustrated with her school work.

_____

_____

Name of the individual(s) who provided this information:

Michelle Boncha Date 4/21/98

Helen Nguyen Date 4-21-98

20. Does this student speak English as a second language or have limited English proficiency?

☒ Yes ☐ No

If yes, does or has this student received ESL/LEP support services?

☒ Yes ☐ No

21a. Do you or the parents/guardians have reason to believe this student has a poor self-concept?

☒ Yes   ☐ No   ☐ Unsure at this time

If yes or unsure at this time, please comment: Mrs. Cole believes Lisa's poor self-concept stems from being over weight and being unsuccessful with her school work.

21b. If the answer was "Yes" or unsure at this time" to question number 21a, do you or the parents/guardians believe this student's poor self-concept is directly related to the student's school difficulty?

☒ Yes   ☐ No   ☐ Unsure at this time

If yes or unsure at this time, please comment: We both believe her school struggles are the root cause of her lack of confidence.

Name of the individual(s) who provided this information: Helen Nguyen Date 4-21-98
Willa Cole, Counselor Date 4-21-98

22. Check all intervention programs and services that have been tried with this student to date:

☐ Accelerated learning   ☒ Remediation
☒ Counseling   ☒ Summer school(s)
☐ Special education   ☒ Title I support
☐ Private tutoring   ☒ In-school tutoring
☒ ESL/LEP   ☐ Speech/language support services

☐ Other _____
☐ Other _____

Please comment on the results of these interventions/ programs and services: Mrs. Cole reports that Lisa's most positive school connection is with her peer group. The ESL/LEP & academic interventions help Lisa maintain her current skill levels, but she is not showing strong growth in these areas.

23. What classroom accommodations and modifications have been made to date? Extra art time has been helpful to Lisa's attitude towards school. She also has responded well when her assignments have been shortened and when she can answer orally instead of writing.

Please comment on the results of these classroom adaptations. As noted above adaptations are seen as key components to Lisa's success in school. These will need to be continued & assessed frequently to ensure an appropriate learning environment for Lisa.

24. Please list additional interventions programs and services that will be provided for this student next year: We recommend: ① Curriculum modifications to help achieve attainable goals ② Instructional accomodations to help improve Lisa's spelling, reading & knowledge of math facts ③ additional intervention services through the reading specialist.

Health/Well-Being
(Optional Questions)

Questions 25-43 cover what may be considered private family matters. Due to the extremely sensitive nature of these questions confidentiality must be protected. Information provided by parents/guardians should only be available to the child study team. **Parents/guardians are not required to answer any of these questions.**

25a. Is this student's physical development within the normal range for his/her age as determined by a physician?

☐ Yes ☒ No

If no, please comment: Lisa is considered big for her age as determined by Mrs. Davidson the school nurse

25b. Do you or the parents/guardians think this student is physically: (check one)

☐ Average size for his/her age?
☐ Small for his/her age?
☒ Large for his/her age?

Comments: Lisa is one of the largest girls in her class.

Name of the individual(s) who provided this information:

Michelle Boucher Date 4/21/98
Helen Nguyen Date 4-21-98

26. Does this student have serious medical problems, such as:

Insulin deficient diabetes? ☐ Yes ☒ No
Asthma? ☒ Yes ☐ No
Allergies? ☐ Yes ☒ No

Other? (please specify) _____

If yes to any of the above, please comment: Lisa has had asthma since she was four years old.

Name of the individual(s) who provided this information:

Helen Nguyen Date 4-21-98
_____ Date _____

27. Has this student had any serious childhood illnesses such as:

Encephalitis? ☐ Yes ☒ No
Spinal meningitis? ☐ Yes ☒ No
Whooping cough? ☐ Yes ☒ No

Other? (please specify) _____

If yes to any of the above, please comment: _____

Name of the individual(s) who provided this information:

Helen Nguyen Date 4-21-98
_____ Date _____

28. Has this student ever suffered a serious childhood accident?

☐ Yes ☒ No

If yes, please comment: _____

Name of the individual(s) who provided this information:

Helen Nguyen Date 4-21-98
_____ Date _____

29. Has this child ever been exposed to toxic substances such as lead, pesticides, inhalants, etc.?

☐ Yes   ☒ No

If yes please comment: _____

_____

_____

_____

_____

Name of the individual(s) who provided this information:

Helen Nguyen _____ Date 4-21-98

_____ Date _____

30. Do you or the parents/guardians suspect this student has:

Vision problems?   ☐ Yes ☒ No ☐ Unsure

Auditory problems? ☐ Yes ☒ No ☐ Unsure

If yes or unsure, please comment: _____

_____

_____

_____

_____

_____

Name of the individual(s) who provided this information:

Helen Nguyen _____ Date 4-21-98

_____ Date _____

31. Does this student have a serious physical disability?

☐ Yes   ☒ No

If yes, please comment: _____

_____

_____

_____

_____

_____

Name of the individual(s) who provided this information:

Helen Nguyen _____ Date 4-21-98

_____ Date _____

32. Does this student's family live at or below the poverty level?

☒ Yes   ☐ No

If yes, please comment: Lisa's mother works very hard but does not make enough money to cover the bills. They currently receive public assistance.

Name of the individual(s) who provided this information:

Helen Nguyen _____ Date 4-21-98

Michelle Bonchu _____ Date 4/21/98

33. Was this child's birth considered traumatic/difficult?

☒ Yes   ☐ No

If yes, please comment: Mrs. Nguyen says Lisa didn't breathe right away.

Name of the individual(s) who provided this information:

Helen Nguyen _____ Date 4-21-98

_____ Date _____

34. Was this child born with a low birthweight?

☒ Yes   ☐ No

If yes, please check:

☒ Low birthweight (5.5 lbs. or less)

☐ Very low birthweight (approximately 3.5 lbs. or less)

Comments: Lisa was born with a low birthweight, but Mrs. Nguyen is unable to recall the exact weight.

Name of the individual(s) who provided this information:

Helen Nguyen _____ Date 4-21-98

_____ Date _____

35. Was this child born prematurely?

[X] Yes [ ] No

If yes, please check:

[X] Premature

[ ] Extremely premature (approximately 25 weeks or less)

Comments: Mrs. Nguyen says Lisa was born 5 weeks early and she thinks the due date was around 3/6/90

Name of the individual(s) who provided this information: *Helen Nguyen* Date 4-21-98

_____ Date _____

36. During the pregnancy, was the mother:
(check all that apply)

A. [ ] Abusing drugs/alcohol?

B. [X] Smoking/exposed to secondhand smoke?

C. [ ] Malnourished?

D. [ ] Exposed to toxic substances (i.e., lead, pesticides, inhalants, etc.)?

E. [X] Experiencing extreme stress (i.e., traumatized by divorce, abuse, poverty, etc.)?

F. [ ] Other (please specify): _____

Please comment on any factors or circumstances checked: Mrs. Nguyen states her boyfriend exposed her to second hand smoke during her pregnancy. She feels his smoking aggravates Lisa's asthma. She feels stressed living in a "slum" neighborhood.

Name of the individual(s) who provided this information: *Helen Nguyen* Date 4-21-98

_____ Date _____

37. Has this child ever suffered from malnutrition?

[ ] Yes [X] No

If yes, please comment: _____

_____

_____

_____

_____

_____

_____

Name of the individual(s) who provided this information: *Helen Nguyen* Date 4-21-98

_____ Date _____

38. Has this child had a traumatic experience such as:

Someone close to the child has died?

[ ] Yes [X] No

The child has witnessed or has been the victim of a violent act?

[X] Yes [ ] No

The child's family was or is in crisis?
(For example, going through a divorce)

[ ] Yes [X] No

Moving to a new home?

[ ] Yes [X] No

Someone close to the child was (or is) terminally ill or injured?

[ ] Yes [X] No

Other (please specify) _____

If yes to any of the above, please comment: Mrs. Nguyen's boyfriend used to hit her in front of Lisa.

_____

_____

_____

Name of the individual(s) who provided this information: *Helen Nguyen* Date 4-21-98

_____ Date _____

39a. Do you or the parents/guardians suspect this child may be suffering from depression?

☐ Yes   ☐ No   ☒ Unsure at this time

If unsure at this time, please comment: _____

_____

_____

_____

39b. If the answer to question number 39a was "Yes," what signs of depression does this child display?

Often seems sad	☒ Yes	☐ No
Does not seem to have fun or enjoy school	☒ Yes	☐ No
Does not want to participate in activities	☒ Yes	☐ No
Prefers to be alone	☒ Yes	☐ No
Lacks enthusiasm	☒ Yes	☐ No

Please comment: Lisa often feels sad and withdrawn. This may be because she is struggling in school

_____

_____

Name of the individual(s) who provided this information:

Michelle Boucher _____ Date 4/21/98

Helen Nguyen _____ Date 4-21-98

40. Have you or the parents/guardians noticed this student displaying any signs of emotional problems such as:

Frequent, uncontrollable outbursts?	☐ Yes	☐ No
Withdrawn, unable to relate to others?	☐ Yes	☐ No
Frequent lying to parents/guardians?	☒ Yes	☐ No

Other? _____

If yes, please comment: Lisa lies to her mother about her school work and her class performance.

Name of the individual(s) who provided this information:

Helen Nguyen _____ Date 4-21-98

_____ Date _____

41. Do you or the parents/guardians think this student exhibits any serious behavior problems such as:

Frequent defiance of adults?	☒ Yes	☐ No
Aggressive/violent behavior towards others?	☐ Yes	☒ No
Frequent use of inappropriate language?	☐ Yes	☒ No

Other? (please specify) _____

If yes, please comment: She is defiant at home, but not at school.

_____

_____

_____

Name of the individual(s) who provided this information:

Helen Nguyen _____ Date 4-21-98

_____ Date _____

42. Do you or the parents/guardians feel this student exhibits signs of social problems such as:

Being unable to make or keep friends?	☐ Yes	☒ No
Does not get along with his/her peer group?	☐ Yes	☒ No
Has difficulty sharing/taking turns?	☐ Yes	☒ No
Tends to say or do inappropriate things?	☐ Yes	☒ No

If yes, please comment: _____

_____

_____

_____

_____

Name of the individual(s) who provided this information:

Helen Nguyen _____ Date 4-21-98

_____ Date _____

43. What other issues should the child study team consider (siblings, is this a foster child, etc.)? _____

_N/A_

_____

_____

_____

End of Optional Health/Well-Being Questions

44. What is this student's attitude toward remaining at the same grade level an additional year?

Student supports staying at the same grade level for an additional year.

☐ Yes ☒ No ☐ Unsure at this time

Student is opposed to staying at the same grade level for an additional year.

☒ Yes ☐ No ☐ Unsure at this time

Comments: _Lisa does not want to stay back. She is adamant about this._

_____

_____

45. What is this student's attitude toward being promoted to the next grade?

Student supports being promoted to the next grade.

☒ Yes ☐ No ☐ Unsure at this time

Student is opposed to being promoted to the next grade.

☐ Yes ☒ No ☐ Unsure at this time

Comments: _Lisa wants to stay with her friends._

_____

_____

46. How do the parents/guardians feel about having their child remain at the same grade level for an additional year?

☐ They support their child remaining at the same grade level an additional year.

☒ They are unsure at this time about having their child remain at the same grade level an additional year.

☐ They are opposed to having their child remain at the same grade level an additional year.

Comments: _Mrs. Nguyen does not know what to do. She will go along with the school's recommendation._

_____

_____

Name of the individual(s) who provided this information: _Helen Nguyen_ Date _4-21-98_

_____ Date _____

47. How do the parents/guardians feel about their child being promoted?

☐ They support their child being promoted to the next grade.

☒ They are unsure at this time about having their child being promoted to the next grade.

☐ They are opposed to having their child being promoted to the next grade.

Comments: _____

_____

_____

_____

_____

_____

_____

Name of the individual(s) who provided this information: _Helen Nguyen_ Date _4-21-98_

_____ Date _____

48. The child study team members believe that this student should be:

☑ Promoted ☐ Retained ☐ Unsure at this time
Principal _Susan Scott_

☑ Promoted ☐ Retained ☐ Unsure at this time
Teacher(s) _Michelle Boucher_

☒ Promoted ☐ Retained ☐ Unsure at this time
School counselor _Willie Cole_

☒ Promoted ☐ Retained ☐ Unsure at this time
School psychologist _John Wilmes_

☐ Promoted ☒ Retained ☐ Unsure at this time
Learning specialist _Chris Owens_

☑ Promoted ☐ Retained ☐ Unsure at this time
Child study team leader _Susan Scott_

☐ Promoted ☐ Retained ☒ Unsure at this time
Other _Marcus Jackson — Reading Specialist_

☐ Promoted ☐ Retained ☐ Unsure at this time
Other _____

☐ Promoted ☐ Retained ☐ Unsure at this time
Other _____

Comments: _____
_____
_____

RECOMMENDATION

49. The child study team recommends that this student:

A. ☒ Be promoted to the next grade level and receive support services such as remediation, accelerated learning, summer school, etc.

B. ☐ Be promoted to the next grade level and stay with the same teacher in a looping configuration.

C. ☐ Be placed in a transition grade/program (i.e., pre-kindergarten, pre-first, pre-second, pre-third).

D. ☐ Remain another year at the same grade level with the same teacher.

E. ☐ Remain another year at the same grade level, but with a different teacher.

F. ☐ Remain another year at the same grade level, but in a different school setting. (This option may not be possible in some school systems.)

G. ☐ Remain an additional year in a multiage classroom.

H. ☐ Be re-placed back one grade level mid-year.

I. ☐ Other (please specify): _____
_____

Comments: _This fall Lisa will be in Michael Johnson's fourth grade class. Michael is going to "loop" with his class and stay with them until the end of fifth grade. Lisa should benefit from being in a stable classroom environment for two years._

50. The child study team is encouraged to create and implement either an Individual Retention Plan (IRP) or Individual Promotion Plan (IPP) for this student. This good faith plan is a non-binding, non-legal agreement created by the child study team focusing on identified goals to ensure school success for this student. This individual plan outlines a course of action that specifies what intervention programs, services and adaptations will be implemented, who will take responsibility to see that it happens as well as when they will happen. **The child study team recommends an:**

☐ Individual Retention Plan   ☒ Individual Promotion Plan   ☐ IRP/IPP is not necessary at this time

If a plan is to be created and implemented, who will be the child study team person responsible for managing the plan?

Susan Scott   _Principal_
Name   Title/Role

The child study team will meet again on _Sept. 22_ to follow up on this student's progress.

Retention / Promotion Checklist:
Summary & Recommendations

> The following summary is based on information and observations from the checklist as documented by parents/guardians and school personnel.
>
> The school believes student placement decisions should be made on an informed, individual basis.
>
> Any decision will have pros and cons for the student. These factors are weighed to make a placement recommendation that is in the best interest of the individual student. Along with the placement recommendation, an Individual Retention Plan (IRP) or an Individual Promotion Plan (IPP) is included where appropriate. The IRP or IPP is a plan of action for each student that includes program interventions and services, including instructional accommodations and curriculum modifications.

Student Name: __Lisa Nguyen__ Date: __5/7/98__ School Year: __1998-99__

Placement Recommendation: (see attached summary)

| | Retention | Individual Retention Plan | Yes | No |

☐ **Retention** **Individual Retention Plan** Yes No

☑ **Promotion** **Individual Promotion Plan** (Yes) No

Next year's teacher: __Michael Johnson- Grade 4 Teacher (with looping) He will progress to 5th grade with this class.__

Summary prepared by: __Susan Scott, Principal__

I/We accept/reject this recommendation:

Helen Nguyen   _4-28-98_
Signature of parent/guardian   Date

_____   _____
Signature of parent/guardian   Date

Retention / Promotion Checklist:
Summary & Recommendations For

Lisa Nguyen

Student's Name

PROS	CONS
1. Lisa is adamant that she does not want to stay back.	1. Lisa is a year and a half below grade level in reading; her math skills are at a beginning 3rd grade level.
2. She wants to be with her friends in 4th grade.	2. She frequently does not complete school work.
3. She is large in size for her age.	3. She complains that the work is too hard.
4. Her performance on an individual intelligence test (with LEP support) shows below average potential.	4. She is a "limited-English proficient" student.
5. Socially/emotionally, she is most positive when with her peers.	

Comments: The team agrees that Lisa's recommendation is a difficult one. Academically, she is performing below grade level in all of her subject areas. She also lacks confidence and cries frequently. The question is whether or not retaining Lisa in third grade will help her improve academically. The team agrees that retention in 3rd grade will neither change or improve Lisa's circumstances. Her attitude is of critical concern in this area. Lisa's own strong objections to retention need to be respected. The team believes the most positive decision for Lisa is to promote her to Michael Johnson's class. He will loop to 5th grade with Lisa's class. She should also attend summer school and receive a full special education evaluation before fall and receive the support outlined in her IPP.

Individual Promotion Plan (IPP)

Student **Lisa Nguyen** (Name)   Date of Birth **1/26/89**

Present Grade Placement **3rd grade**   Date **4/28/98**

Placement Recommendation (grade level/program) **4th grade**

School **Central School**   Phone **474-7918**

Parent(s)/Guardian(s) **Helen Nguyen** Name(s)

Mailing Address **PO Box 63**   Phone **474-9519**

Child Study Team Manager **Susan Scott**   Title/Role **Principal**

Principal **Susan Scott** Name

Classroom Teacher(s) **Michelle Boucher** Name(s)

Parent(s)/Guardian(s) Approval   ☒ I/we approve this IPP

☐ I/we do not approve this IPP

Parent(s)/Guardian(s) Signature **Helen Nguyen**   Date **4/28/98**

Parent(s)/Guardian(s) Signature _____   Date _____

The undersigned individuals participated in the writing of this IPP

Name	Title/Role	Date
Susan Scott	Principal/Child Study Team Manager	4-27-98
Michelle Boucher	3rd grade teacher	4/28/98
Willa Cox	Counselor	4-28-98
Michael Johnson	4TH GR TEACHER	4-28-98
John Witmer	School psychologist	4-28-98

Student **Lisa Nguyen**   Date **4/28/98**

Additional Intervention Programs and Services (IPP)

	Progress Review
Goal: She will recognize 3rd grade sightwords ǂ be reading at a 2.6 level by June, 1999.	Date: _____
Intervention/Services: Reading support Lisa will be referred for a full evaluation to screen for any learning disabilities. She will continue receiving ½ hr. daily in class reading support through Title One.	Comments: _____ _____ _____ _____ _____ _____
Implemented by: Marcus Jackson	
Title/Role: Reading Specialist	
Goal: She will master addition ǂ subtraction facts and know multiplication tables through 5 by June, 1999.	Progress Review
Intervention/Services: Remedial math support Lisa will receive ½ hr. daily in class math support in a small group setting.	Date: _____ Comments: _____ _____ _____ _____ _____
Implemented by: Leona Carle	
Title/Role: Remedial specialist	
Goal: Support her on going reading and math progress.	Progress Review
Intervention/Services: Summer School She will attend a 3 week summer school. The morning will focus on math and reading, Afternoon will focus on the arts.	Date: _____ Comments: _____ _____ _____ _____ _____
Implemented by: _____	
Title/Role: _____	

Student: **Lisa Nguyen**   Date **4/28/98**

Instructional Accommodations (IPP)

Goal: **To Learn Dolch Words**

Accommodations: **Dolch words will be her spelling words. These will be learned through daily games, flash cards and audio cassettes.**

Implemented by: **Marcus Jackson**

Title/Role: **Reading Specialist**

Progress Review

Date: _____

Comments: _____
_____
_____
_____
_____
_____
_____

Goal: **To do problem solving without the language/reading barrier.**

Accommodations: **Story problems will be on tape along with addition and subtraction facts and multiplication tables.**

Implemented by: **Leona Carle**

Title/Role: **remedial specialist**

Progress Review

Date: _____

Comments: _____
_____
_____
_____
_____
_____
_____
_____

Goal: **To deal with the language and reading barrier.**

Accommodations: **She will be provided talking books of her choice**

Implemented by: **Marcus Jackson**

Title/Role: **Reading Specialist**

Progress Review

Date: _____

Comments: _____
_____
_____
_____
_____
_____
_____

Student __Lisa Nguyen__ Date: __4/28/98__

Curriculum Modifications (IPP)

Goal: _To provide an appropriate work load in math and reading._

Modifications: _Her volume of work will be reduced to a manageable level._

Implemented by: _Michael Johnson_

Title/Role: _Lisa's teacher next year_

Progress Review

Date: _____

Comments: _____

Goal: _To create art opportunities as an incentitive to complete school assignments._

Modifications: _Provide two additional art periods per week on an earned basis._

Implemented by: _Michael Johnson_

Title/Role: _Lisa's teacher next year._

Progress Review

Date: _____

Comments: _____

Goal: _To create a realistic approach to address 4th grade standards._

Modifications: _The 4th grade standards will be read to Lisa and she will answer them orally. She will be given additional time to process the answers._

Implemented by: _Michael Johnson_

Title/Role: _Lisa's teacher next year_

Progress Review

Date: _____

Comments: _____

Bibliography

Ames, Louise Bates. *What Am I Doing in This Grade?* Rosemont, NJ: Modern Learning Press, 1985.

American Association of School Administrators. *The Nongraded Primary: Making Schools Fit Children.* Arlington, VA, 1992.

Anderson, Robert H., and Pavan, Barbara Nelson. *Nongradedness: Helping It to Happen.* Lancaster, PA: Technomic Press, 1992.

Boyer, Ernest. *The Basic School: A Community for Learning.* Ewing, NJ: Carnegie Foundation for the Advancement of Learning, 1995.

————. *Ready to Learn: A Mandate for the Nation.* Princeton, NJ: The Foundation for the Advancement of Teaching, 1991.

Brazelton, T. Berry. *To Listen to a Child: Understanding the Normal Problems of Growing Up.* Reading, MA: Addison-Wesley, 1986.

————. *Touchpoints: The Essential Reference. Your Child's Emotional and Behavioral Development.* Reading, MA: Addison-Wesley, 1994.

Carbo, Marie. *Reading Styles Inventory Manual.* Roslyn Heights, New York: National Reading Styles Institute, 1991.

Carbo, Marie; Dunn, Rita; and Dunn, Kenneth. *Teaching Students to Read Through Their Individual Learning Styles.* Needham Heights, MA: Allyn & Bacon, 1991.

Clay, Marie. *Becoming Literate.* Portsmouth, NH: Heinemann, 1991.

————. *Observing Young Readers.* Portsmouth, NH: Heinemann, 1982.

————. *Reading Recovery: A Guidebook for Teachers in Training.* Portsmouth, NH: Heinemann, 1993.

Coletta, Anthony. *Kindergarten Readiness Checklist for Parents.* Rosemont, NJ: Modern Learning Press, 1991.

————. *What's Best for Kids: A Guide to Developmentally Appropriate Practices for Teachers and Parents of Children Age 4–8.* Rosemont, NJ: Modern Learning Press, 1991.

Elkind, David. *All Grown Up & No Place to Go.* Reading, MA: Addison-Wesley, 1984.

————. *The Hurried Child.* Reading, MA: Addison-Wesley, 1981.

————. *Miseducation: Preschoolers at Risk.* New York: Alfred A. Knopf, 1987.

————. *Reinventing Childhood.* Rosemont, NJ: Modern Learning Press, 1998.

Grant, Jim. *Developmental Education in the 1990's.* Rosemont, NJ: Modern Learning Press, 1991.

————. *"I Hate School!" Some Common-Sense Answers for Educators & Parents Who Want to Know Why and What to Do About It.* Rosemont, NJ: Programs for Education, 1994.

————. *Retention and Its Prevention: Making Informed Decisions About Individual Children.* Rosemont, NJ: Modern Learning Press, 1997.

Grant, Jim, and Johnson, Bob. *A Common Sense Guide to Multiage Practices.* Columbus, OH: Teachers' Publishing Group, 1995.

Grant, Jim; Johnson, Bob; and Richardson, Irv. *The Looping Handbook: Teachers and Students Progressing Together.* Peterborough, NH: Crystal Springs Books, 1996.

————. *Multiage Q&A: 101 Practical Answers to Your Most Pressing Questions.* Peterborough, NH: Crystal Springs Books, 1995.

————. *Our Best Advice: The Multiage Problem Solving Handbook.* Peterborough, NH: Crystal Springs Books, 1996.

Grant, Jim, and Richardson, Irv, compilers. *Multiage Handbook: A Comprehensive Resource for Multiage Practices.* Peterborough, NH: Crystal Springs Books, 1996.

Goodman, Gretchen. *I Can Learn! Strategies and Activities for Gray-Area Children.* Peterborough, NH: Crystal Springs Books, 1995.

————. *More I Can Learn!* Peterborough, NH: Crystal Springs Books, 1997.

————. *Inclusive Classrooms from A to Z: A Handbook for Educators.* Columbus, OH: Teachers' Publishing Group, 1994.

Healy, Jane M. *Endangered Minds: Why Children Don't Think and What We Can Do About It.* New York: Simon and Schuster, 1990.

————. *Your Child's Growing Mind: A Guide to Learning and Brain Development From Birth to Adolescence.* New York: Doubleday, 1987.

Hobby, Janice Hale. *Staying Back.* Gainesville, FL: Triad, 1990.

Mallory, Bruce, and New, Rebecca, eds. *Diversity and Developmentally Appropriate Practices: Challenges for Early Childhood Education.* New York: Teachers College Press, 1994.

Miller, Karen. *Ages and Stages: Developmental Descriptions and Activities Birth Through Eight Years.* Chelsea, MA: Telshare Publishing Co., 1985.

National Education Commission on Time and Learning. *Prisoners of Time.* Washington, DC: U.S. Government Printing Office, Superintendent of Documents, 1994.

Pavelka, Patricia. *Making the Connection: Learning Skills Through Literature.* Peterborough, NH: Crystal Springs Books, 1995.

Payne, Ruby K. *Poverty: A Framework: Understanding and Working with Students and Adults From Poverty.* Baytown, TX: RFT Publishing, 1995.

Phinney, Margaret. *Reading with the Troubled Reader.* Portsmouth, NH: Heinemann, 1989.

Rhodes, Lynn, and Dudley-Marling, Curtis. *Readers and Writers with a Difference: A Holistic Approach to Teaching Learning Disabled and Remedial Students.* Portsmouth: Heinemann, 1988.

Rosner, Jerome. *Helping Children Overcome Learning Difficulties.* New York: Walker and Co., 1979.

Uphoff, James K. *Real Facts From Real Schools: What You're Not Supposed To Know About School Readiness and Transition Programs.* Rosemont, NJ: Modern Learning Press, 1990, 1995.

Uphoff, James, K.; Gilmore, June; and Huber, Rosemarie. *Summer Children: Ready (or Not) for School.* Middletown, OH: The Oxford Press, 1986.

Wood, Chip. *Yardsticks: Children in the Classroom Ages 4-12.* Greenfield, MA: Northeast Foundation for Children, 1994.

Audio/Video

Grant, Jim. *Accommodating Developmentally Different Children in the Multiage Classroom*, 1993. Keynote address at the NAESP Annual Convention. Audiocassette available from Chesapeake Audio/Video Communications, Inc. (6330 Howard Lane, Elkridge, MD 21227, product #180).

———. *Do You Know Where Your Child Is?* Video, 1985. Modern Learning Press.

———. *Grade Replacement.* Audiotape. Modern Learning Press.

———. *Jim Grant Live.* Audiotape. Modern Learning Press, 1985.

———. *Making Informed Decisions About Retention.* Audiotape, 1998. Crystal Springs Books.

———. *The Looping Video with Char Forsten and Jim Grant.* Peterborough, NH: Crystal Springs Books, Video, 1998.

———. *Worth Repeating.* Video. Modern Learning Press.

Goodman, Gretchen. *Classroom Strategies for "Gray-Area" Children.* Peterborough, NH: Crystal Springs Books, 1995. Video.